# You Don't Have to Live In The Past:

## How I Found Peace Through Life's Struggles and Pain

Jon Wilson

The author can be contacted by email at jonwilson7743@gmail.com

# You Don't Have to Live In The Past:
## How I Found Peace Through Life's Struggles and Pain

### By Jon Christopher Wilson
With André Bernier

# Chapter 1:
# Birth Parents

My name is Jon Christopher Wilson. I was born in South Korea on March 2, 1975. This is the date that was given to me by the administrators of the orphanage. In reality, I was living on the streets until a police officer caught me and brought me to an orphanage. They tried to find a birth certificate but one was never found.

Before my journey of living on the run and on the streets, life was as normal as could be. Until I was three years old, I had a place that I called home with parents that made the very best of a small, one-room house. That one-room house had a charcoal stove on which my mother cooked. At night, all of us including my grandmother slept on the floor. Despite sounding like a bleak existence, we were all happy. My surviving memory of that period is a pleasant one. I was a normal and happy child surrounded by loving parents.

I was closest to my mother since my father was away much of the time. Even though my grandmother lived with us, I do not have many clear memories of her except for the time that she sat me down and gave me an apple. Other random memories from those first three years include being given animal crackers to eat every morning, sleeping close to my mother's side every night and being shown so much love and attention. Basically, my life in those early years were all very happy until that fateful day when my world was suddenly turned upside-down. That was the day that my parents abandoned me.

# Chapter 2:
# Separation and Abandonment

The day started like any other. It was a beautiful day. The sun was shining, the birds were singing, and the leaves were turning colors. There wasn't a single cloud in the sky that day. As much as a three-year-old child can understand, I felt so fortunate to have wonderful parents who loved me and made me so happy. I was riding high on top of my father's shoulders as my parents told me that we were going to a friend's house for a visit. How could a day like this be anything less than perfect?

All of those beautiful feelings and emotions which felt like they reached invincibly high into the deep, blue sky, came crashing down in the matter of minutes. My parents met someone in the road that I had never seen. I don't remember much about their exchange, but I do remember the tidal wave of panic when I saw my father and mother walking away from me. What was all of this about? This other woman, whom I did not know, had a strong grasp on me. I tried desperately to escape from that grasp as my parents disappeared down the road. I cried and yelled out to them as loudly as I could but it had no effect. Why were they leaving me? Was it just for a moment? Was it just a temporary visit with their so-called friends? It didn't matter at that moment. I wanted to be with my father and mother.

Once it became apparent to my three-year old mind that my parents were not coming back, I remember crying all of that day and all of that night. My heart felt so empty that I felt as though nothing could ever fill it. That emptiness grew every single day. The only thing in my life that ever made me feel safe and happy was gone. Even though there were people around me, the loneliness was overwhelming. The only grain of hope that remained was that my parents would return in the morning. After crying myself to sleep, I woke the next morning running to the door to wait for them, but they never returned for me. Why did they leave me? Was it because we were so poor that they could no longer afford to keep me? So many of those questions still remain to this day. Perhaps someday with enough time and money, I will search for those answers.

The place where my parents left me was a Buddhist monastery for monks. I stayed with the couple who lived there as resident caretaker. For a three-year-old kid, the monastery was a curious place surrounded by its high, stone walls. There was a gargantuan wooden door that served as the entrance and exit. Many people came to visit especially during certain Buddhist celebrations and ceremonies at specific times on their religious calendar. I can remember times when I would wander through the monastery to explore, finding all kinds of statues and other structures of antiquity throughout the place.

I was given a job. I had to sweep the floors near and around the front gate every single day. That was a joy compared to what I had to endure at other times. At night, I slept on a cold floor near my caretaker's mother. I was always frightened of her so we hardly ever said a word to one another. But even that was far better than the treatment I received from my caretaker. Simply put, she was mean. Whenever I did anything that displeased her, I had to go outside and break off a branch that she would then use to swat my thighs. She had children of her own but I don't remember being able to play with them very much. To my little mind, there was no kindness anywhere in her heart. Not once did she ever show me reason to believe that she even remotely cared for me. This is what I lived with for days, weeks, and months.

By the time I turned five years old, I began attending school. It was there that I began to experience things that began to slowly restore my trust in other people. I remember being excited to learn how to read and write, and do math problems. Every morning before classes began, the principal of the school would gather all of the students outside to do daily stretches and exercises. While I was enjoying this new experience, I was shy and was not able to make many friends easily. Despite the new academic work that challenged me, I was still preoccupied with thinking about where my parents were, wondering if they were even thinking about me.

Finally, after a little while, I did make friends with another boy who lived in the neighborhood. He lived so close to me at the monastery that I would spend much of my time at his house. There, we played with his toys as I filled my stomach with animal crackers that his mother gave to us. This brought to mind the animal crackers that my mother would give to me when we were living a simple, happy life together. In a strange way, it was a very, very small restoration of the things that I longed for. We did nearly everything together. It was almost as if I was a special part of this family. That gave me the license to think about what "normal" little boys think about instead of being obsessed with where my parents were. Finally, I was happy again.

Just when things had settled into a routine that I could live with, another emotional tsunami was ready to overtake me without warning. The day started like every other day. School was first. Then I walked to my friend's house. As I walked into my friend's home, I instantly knew that something was wrong. I was right. My friend's parents sat me down and told me news that I simply did not want to hear or believe. They were moving away. Most of their belongings had been packed up and shipped out. I spent as much time as I could with my special friend until it was time for his family to leave. When it was time to say goodbye, all of the wounds of being abandoned that had partially healed over time had burst open with force. Why was this happening again? The blurred, teary-eyed image of my friend waving at me from his back window of his car as they pulled away is forever burned in my memory. My tears were unstoppable. My heart had been crushed once again. My parents had abandoned me. Now my best friend and his parents were abandoning me. Any light that managed to work back into the depths of my spirit over a few years had been completely extinguished. I was alone again. Perpetual sadness became my constant companion.

I started to wonder if this would be the pattern of my life. Why was I being abandoned by the people that I loved and to whom I was close? Would everyone in my future leave me too? These are things that a five-year-old boy should never have to ponder.

I began thinking more and more about my parents again. I held onto the slimmest chance that they would someday return to the monastery to to get me so that we could return to the days of being a happy family. I waited for them every day. The cold wooden floor became a place that I once again cried myself to sleep almost every night.

In the months that followed, I would occasionally take it upon myself to go to the local police department. Surely they would help me find my parents. I was wrong. The only thing they did was to return me to the monastery, a place I associated with being beaten by a mean lady.

The time came when I realized that my parents were not going to come back for me. I decided that I needed to take matters into my own hand. While I didn't have a specific plan on how I was going to find my parents, I needed to strike out on my own to start the process of looking for them.

When that day came, I pretended to prepare like it was any other school day. At the right moment, I hid myself in the monastery and patiently waited for everyone inside to leave. When I was convinced that everyone was gone, I made my move. Without the luxury of packing anything, I pushed open the large wooden doors with nothing more than the clothes on my back. Once outside, I felt free. I never looked back. No more mean lady. No more branches striking my thighs. No more sleeping on a cold floor with someone who didn't really care about me. I wanted leave all of those terrible memories in that monastery as I walked away from that place.

As I watched all of the activity buzzing about me, I saw a world of excitement. I loved to explore the monastery when I first arrived there, but exploring a wide-open world offered limitless possibilities. At the very same time, other less inviting thoughts ran in the background. Where would my next meal come from? Would I starve? Would I get sick? With what kinds of dangers would I have to deal? How cold would the air be tonight? Would loneliness get the best of me? After a while, I was overwhelmed with the implications of the escape I had just executed, but I truly did not care. I was convinced that I would now be able to find my parents and that life would return to the happy normal I remember from years before.

# Chapter 3:
# Running Away

The world seemed so big and so exciting as I began my quest to find my parents. Years of living life in the monastery did not diminish my desire to be reunited with them. I never stopped needing their love. I never stopped needing the safety and happiness that they provided for me. Those deep-seated desires helped me to deal with many of the issues of being a street kid.

The first issue began early in my meanderings and it followed me wherever I went. Hunger became a constant companion and drove me to do things that most people would not even consider. Every once in awhile, I would see a piece of food on the ground or inside a trash can. It did not matter how long it had been there or how it looked or smelled. If it was food, I claimed it and ate it. It was what I had to do to survive physically so that I could continue on my mission. That mission kept me alive.

At some point many weeks into my existence as a street kid, I stumbled upon a church where there appeared to be something important happening. In a very matter-of-fact way, I made my way closer and sat beside a man and asked him what was going on. He said that there was a wedding going on. I had no idea

what a wedding was, but I was curious enough to
march up the stairs where to a room that was large with
many people smiling and having a good time. What
really amazed me was the abundance of food
everywhere! I was so hungry that I did not think twice
about running up to the banquet table to eat. I
constantly wondered if anyone would scold me or stop
me, but no one did. I kept eating. I ate until I was
completely stuffed. It was wonderful. Feeling satisfied,
I walked back downstairs and back into the street to
resume looking for my parents.

My search soon led me to a train station where
the daily frenzy of people scurrying to and fro amazed
and entertained me. Who were all these people? Where
were they all going? Amidst the controlled chaos, I saw
a bench in the distance. I walked over to it and sat
down. I didn't realize how tired I felt until I sat down
for a moment. I stretched out to close my eyes just for a
moment and fell fast asleep. When I woke, the station
was eerily empty except for a few people here and
there. Feeling hungry, I scraped up any discarded food
that I could find in the trash can and on the floor. There
were a few scraps of very dirty food, but at that point I
could not afford to be choosey.

There was a train in the station that appeared to
be preparing to leave. Without anything to lose, I snuck
onto the train and found a seat next to a stranger. A
sense of adventure came over me as the train pulled
away. We were on our way, but to where? I didn't care.

It was going somewhere. The man next to me didn't seem to mind that I was there. He started asking me all kinds of questions, namely, where my parents were. I was old enough to know that telling him the truth may have resulted in losing the freedom to continue searching for them. I simply shrugged my shoulders.

My attention was drawn to the window. I had never seen so many different things whip by the window at such a high speed. It was yet another new and amazing thing that I was experiencing. Just then, an official looking man in a suit appeared at the front of the train car. He began asking for people's train tickets to punch. When he arrived to our seat, I did not know what to do. The man next to me said something to him. He then punched the man's ticket and moved on. I have no idea how he was able to persuade him to ignore me, but he did. I was so grateful.

When the train stopped, that man next to me asked if I had anywhere to go. When I said no, he invited me to come and stay at his house where his family was. Without any other options, I agreed. Once at his home, the man introduced me to his family. They were kind enough to share their meal with me. My belly was satisfied and it felt good to know that I would not be sleeping in the cold again. They all slept on the floor as I did.

During the night, I woke up and must have been making too much noise for them and they became angry. They actually told me that I would have to leave. Before I had the chance to apologize or protest, I was whisked out their door. Once more, I found myself surrounded by the cold, dark, and damp air. As frightened as I was, I took comfort in two things. The first was how absolutely stunning the stars looked over my head. The second was to think about my parents. After a while of aimless wandering, I became very tired. I found a tree away from the road that I propped myself near where I fell asleep in the cold night air.

As daybreak came, I woke and could hardly move from being so cold. On top of that, I found that I was absolutely filthy from head to toe from being in so many places without ever taking a bath or shower. The odor of urine on me was strong. I must have urinated on myself during the night without my waking up.

I had no other choice but to keep going anywhere to look for food. As I walked toward what seemed to be a small town, I began thinking about my parents again. While thinking of them brought me comfort in the cold, dark night, thinking of them now welled up so much emotion that I began to cry a lot as I walked toward the next small town.

The town had a bus station that was heated. Feeling the warmth of that place was heavenly. My legs were sore from so much walking so I found a bench and sat down for a while before beginning the task of looking for food scraps in the trash bins. When I did muster the strength for sticking my head in the trash barrel, I found scraps of old food that was covered in dirt. I didn't even think about how unappetizing it was. I just ate it. It was something to put in my stomach to satisfy it for a short while.

I found it amazing that no one gave me a second glance. I thought that someone might call the local police or child services, but no one did. Being so tired, I stretched out on one of the benches and fell asleep. When I woke, it was as if someone changed the scene of a play being acted out. There was now a great deal of activity. Buses were filing in and out of the station. I stepped outside and immediately sampled the familiar smell of bus exhaust. Without even thinking about it, I picked a bus and boarded it. Because I was so small, I found my way to the back row undetected. Not even the bus driver noticed me. There was another sense of adventure when we finally pulled away from the bus station. With my little nose pressed up against the glass of the back window, I watched as the scenery went by. After a while, I settled back into my seat. Like a lullabye, the motion of the bus enticed me to close my eyes and I eventually drifted back to sleep.

When I woke, the bus was empty and idling. That's when the bus driver finally noticed me. He asked me where my parents were. Thinking fast, I made up a story. I told him that I lived close by, just up the road to where I was pointing. I must have been convincing because that is where the bus driver stopped and opened up his doors to bid me farewell. Another close call of almost being caught and turned over to the authorities. Now what? I continued doing what I had been since I left the monastery. I just started walking. My mission had not changed. I was searching for my father and mother.

As I approached yet another town, I remember how busy it seemed to be with many people selling different things on the side of the main road. It goes without saying that food was among the things being sold. The aroma was heavenly. It was my lucky day. I found enough on the ground to curb my intense hunger. As I continued to walk down the street, I could not help to notice that there was a truck unloading loaves of freshly baked bread. You could smell it from a distance. I did everything that I could to get close enough to grab one of those loaves while the loaves were being unloaded, but every time that I seemed to have an opportunity, the truck driver returned close to where I was standing.

In the same town, I also wanted to steal a neat bus toy that I saw on display, but there was a giant window that prevented me from even trying. It wasn't food, but it was a toy that reminded me of how desperately I wanted to return to a loving family so that I could just be a carefree kid again. Perhaps it was just as well that I could not steal that toy. It would have simply reminded me that I did not have time to be a kid.

Walking back outside to the street, something on the ground caught my attention. Lying there near a group of workers, there was money, a paper bill. As I approached it, I had no idea how much it was worth. I quickly picked it up before anyone noticed and slipped it into my pocket. Somehow, I knew that what I should do was to ask if anyone lost this money, but as a juvenile nomad, even a kid like me was constantly wondering where my next makeshift meal would come from. To me, it was a gift horse. I finally had some money to buy food! But was it enough? I had no way of finding out other than to pick a grocery store, get what I wanted and try to pay for it at the register. After locating a store, I grabbed some delicious looking snacks and walked to the register. I handed the clerk the bill that was in my pocket and watched his eyes carefully. His eyes looked at the bill and his head cocked and then looked at me. He did not have to say anything. I knew the look. He thought that I stole the money.

"Where do you get this money, kid?"

For a moment, I froze and stared back at the clerk. Without saying a word, I panicked and fled the store as fast as I could. I did not stop until I had run so far away that no one could possibly connect me to the money I left at the grocery store. After I caught my breath and assessed the situation, I went back to what I was doing before. I looked for discarded food on the ground and I ate what I was able to find.

My next opportunity to swipe something that did not belong to me was a bike. It was just sitting there without a lock and without its owner anywhere in sight. I moved carefully toward the bike as I kept watch in every direction. No one was suspicious that I was moving toward it. As I moved closer, I realized that the bike was a little larger than what I was used to handling. I didn't care. It was a chance to cover more miles in my quest to find my parents. I hopped onto the bike and started pedaling. The bike's size was too large for me. As I pedaled, I lost my footing and eventually my balance. The bike and I went tumbling to the ground. Not wanting to be beat by a bike, I hopped back on and pedaled some more. My second attempt at fleeing was not much better and I fell again. Not wanting to admit defeat, I tried one more time and had the same result. The bike was too big for me. I was actually angry at the bike and took my frustration out on the bike by throwing to the ground and walking away.

Not long after, I found one of those toy horses that had wheels on it. It was much more my size. Without an owner nearby, I simply sat on the horse and started to push so hard that I could feel the wind pushing past my little boy face. This was much better and so much more fun than a bike that was too big for me. I was able to ride that horse with my little boy legs going as fast as they could. Since it was not designed to be a toy on which speed was the objective, the friction eroded the wheels to the point where decent speed was no longer possible. I ditched the horse and started walking once more having the same determination that led me to make my escape from the monastery. Thoughts of my parents were never far from my mind. While many other things changed around me, this is one thing which never changed. It was the driving force behind everything I did now. I simply had to find them, somehow, somewhere.

In a very odd and indescribable sense, I knew that God was caring for me even though I was never formally introduced to God or the things of God as a toddler. How else could I explain being able to find what I needed to survive at multiple and pivotal points in my street life? The dirty, slimy food was not something I even thought of. It was food and it filled my stomach. For that I was grateful. I knew I was being watched over and cared for. Not once did I ever think to blame God for my circumstances. Somehow, I knew that He was not responsible for my predicament. More so, I knew that He was helping me to survive the rough life of a street kid. The only way that I was able to ward off dying from starvation, cold, and other evils up to now was by God's help. There was no one else in this world that had any true concern for me except for God, and somewhere my parents. There was a reason, unknown to me, that God was helping me to stay alive, and it gave me what I needed to make it through each day on the street.

# Chapter 4:
# Orphanages

Korean holidays had both benefits and drawbacks. This one was no different. The city in which I walked into was alive with activity. Colorful decorations filled the streets. There were happy families smiling and laughing together as they wandered through the decorated streets. You could see the love beaming out of those parents and onto their children. All the joyful  hustle and bustle initially made me happy inside until I realized that I did not have what those other boys and girls had. I daydreamed about the day when I would find my parents and how much joy I would feel.

While taking in the festive scene, I suddenly began to feel sick. My head started to hurt as well. It must have been apparent since a woman with concern on her face walked over to me and asked if I was all right. Even though I felt sick, I knew that I was hungry. I had nothing to lose so I asked her if she had any food. The concern on her face warmed my heart. Perhaps she actually cared about little me. She invited me to follow her to her house. When we arrived there, she gave me something to eat. All the while, she kept asking lots of questions that did not make much sense to me. I was not able to answer most of them.

The meal I was given was far better than anything I ate for weeks. Despite that, the food made me even more sick, but I tried hiding my nausea and discomfort as best as I was able. It must have worked as she did not say anything.

The lady came to the correct conclusion. I was homeless and living on the street. With the same concern on her face, she began telling me about a place where I would not only have a bed in which to sleep and good food to eat, but it was a place that I would be able to stay. That was an appealing thought. She sealed the deal when she said that there were a lot of other kids there, too. After sleeping in the cold and damp air, and after scourging for filthy morsels of food for what seemed like an eternity, I agreed to go.

The lady took me to my first orphanage. As we walked into the building together, someone official looking came to greet us. They spoke for a few minutes before the lady turned to me and said goodbye with a kind of reassuring smile that I would be in very good hands.

The person in charge of the orphanage brought me to the shower. I had been without a bath or shower for so long that I forgot how good it felt to be clean. After my shower, I had no desire to put on my old, filthy clothes. I was glad that I was given clean clothes to wear and something tasty to eat. I felt strangely at home since there were so many other homeless children there. We were connected by a common bond. More importantly, there was a sense of protective care here as nominal as it was. I could take a breather from the exhaustive task of trying to look for my parents even if it was for a day or two. After my shower and meal, they combed my hair and checked for lice. While they did that, the pain inside my ear was horrible. All that digging uncovered a painful ear infection. It was time to lay low for a few days until I felt strong enough to move on.

When that time came, I did the same thing that I had done before. I found a place to hide while everyone left for the day. After hearing no noises for what seemed like a reasonable amount of time, I bolted for the door. I was out on the street again, searching for my parents. The desire to find them was so strong that I did not seem to care that it meant I would soon be hungry and cold again. That cold and hunger greeted me all too quickly, this time with an illness that made my head hurt more and more with every passing hour. I knew that if I did not do something to get help, that I may not survive.

In my wandering, I spotted another orphanage and I simply walked inside until I was noticed. The people inside didn't say a word. They simply stared at me and I stared at them. Finally, one of them slowly made their way to me and started asking me all kinds of questions. My answer was simple. I was lost and have been living on the streets for a while. I was thankful that they took me in and gave me some food to eat.

After feeling satisfied, I began to look around wondering if I had made a poor choice. This orphanage was dirtier than some of the places I had fallen asleep on the streets. The bedrooms were disgusting with bedding that looked as though it had not been in a washing machine for months, maybe even years. I looked around for the bathroom and could not find it. There was a good reason for that. The bathroom was an outdoor outhouse, large and made of bricks. The soiled bedding should have been a clue as to what I would find in the outhouse. After just one step inside the door, I was horrified. Everything around me was covered with flies and maggots. There was human feces, semi-dried urine, vomit, used toilet paper and all sorts of other trash covering the walls and floors, and even the ceiling! Giant worm-like crawlers slithered to and fro next to my feet. To this day I can say that it was the most frightening place that I ever witnessed.

As horrible as this shockingly gruesome environment was, it was not the worst evil lurking in this orphanage. Virtually every child there was both neglected and abused in every way imaginable. It started with the way the adults treated and abused the children. From there, it trickled down to the bigger, meaner kids who treated the smaller and weaker kids in the very same ways. Think of the worst possible things that could happen to a defenseless child and that could only describe the very beginning of the evil that was rampant in this place. At age six, I was personally exposed to things that no human being should ever have to experience or endure, let alone at six years old. There were other times where I was helpless to come to the aid of those I called friends. Overall, I think you get the picture.

It's not difficult to surmiser that sickness and diseases went along with life in this orphanage. Over time, my health declined. Splitting headaches became more frequent. I could feel my body ignite with fever often, especially at night. There were many endless nights that I cried all night for someone to help me, but no one came. No one truly cared. As much of a survivor as I believed I was, I began to entertain thoughts that I was soon going to die.

During one of those endless nights, I became so hungry that I hunted around the floor for anything to eat. I did find some dried feces. Being so hungry and so sick, I had nothing to lose so I ate it. That made the pain in my head even worse. I began to vomit. Once that started, it wouldn't stop, making the pain in my head unbearable. It was a mad and vicious cycle. Finally, someone noticed that I was deathly sick. They tried to attend to me by giving me something to eat. Invariably, everything I was given came right back out with great force. Only then was I taken to the hospital.

The doctors and nurses had great compassion on me. With patience and loving care that almost seemed foreign to me at this point, I slowly stopped vomiting and the headaches began to abate. Then the doctors explained to me that I had contracted polio from the inhumane conditions at the orphanage. While I grew stronger and stronger every day, my right leg was lagging behind. It seemed to be very weak and often could not support a normal walk. The polio virus would eventually mean that my right leg muscles would not grow to their full potential. To this day, my limp is a constant reminder that the virus was the vehicle through which I was rescued from a certain early death in that house of horrors.

As my health returned, I decided very early on that I would never return to that dreadful orphanage again. When I was strong enough, I plotted my move to leave the hospital and move on. Life on the street was far better than living in a place in which so much evil was concentrated. When no one was looking, I quietly slipped away from my room and walked out of the hospital. I was back on the street. My mission had not changed. I was determined to find my parents.

The routine of living on the streets returned. I was back to eating whatever scraps I could find on the ground, sleeping wherever I could find some shelter, and getting rides on buses and trains to help me to travel to different places. Every time I entered a new town or city, my focus on people's faces was razor sharp. I was hopeful that I would capture a glimpse of my father or mother, but every new place netted the same old result. Nothing.

Somehow, I came across another orphanage. You would think that I would have been so affected by the previous house of horrors that I would have strongly recoiled from it. Somehow, I sensed that it was very different. In hindsight, God's Holy Spirit was leading me here.

This third orphanage, indeed, was different. The children were healthy, smiling and full of life. The adults who ran the orphanage were kind, confident and loving. The place itself was clean and bright. There was plenty of good food, too. The residents raised rabbits for food. While we ate rabbit often, compared to anything I would have found on the ground, it was a delight to my taste buds. I was grateful for such good food.

The freedom to enjoy being young and carefree again was something that took me a little time to fully trust, but the environment was so loving that it did not take me long. Soon, I was prancing off to the local creeks and other public pools to swim with my newfound friends. Then there were special visits. Several times a year, American soldiers, who were stationed in Korea, would come and spend time with us. They would come with new toys to distribute to every boy and girl. Many times, they would sit down and teach us to sing English songs. For the first time in my young life, joy in the true sense of the word returned to my heart and soul. I had not felt this way since the joy and security I felt when I was with my parents.

There was a great deal of simplicity in that joy. Living life on the streets is not simple, and it stands to reason that joy is a luxury that has no room to operate if you are going to survive. The atmosphere here gave me liberty to completely shed my survival instinct and to embrace that simplicity and joy. Because there weren't a lot of toys around, we were encouraged to be resourceful. We made many things out of paper such as homemade kites and airplanes. Sticks that we found were used for cross braces for the kites. Anytime we needed glue, we used small amounts of sticky rice which worked just fine.

I also remember giggling and merry-making with my friends as we were taught how to catch grasshoppers and how to roast them over a fire for a snack. I realize that it may not sound very appetizing to people who are not accustomed to eating very many insects, but I can attest to the fact that the roasted grasshoppers were actually quite tasty. The need for being resourceful also meant that sometimes we would be served some unusual items. The one that I truly did not care for was dog soup.

The joy and security I felt here was truly a breath of fresh air. As good as life was here, I still had the nagging empty feeling of being abandoned by my father and mother. I thought of them often. In time, that insatiable desire to find them began to consume me. As good as life was here, and as dangerous as the streets were outside the protection of the orphanage, I knew what I had to do. It was time to quietly sneak out one day and to devote my attention to my original mission, finding my parents. I had some reservations about leaving, but the quest for my parents was too important to me. I was back on the streets, and back in a lifestyle that made me sad on many levels.

Somehow, I managed to find myself wandering into Seoul. It was such an exciting place with so much hustle and bustle. There seemed to be a slightly better opportunity to find scraps of food compared to other places. What I didn't know was that a policewoman was watching me and must have come to the conclusion that I was a street kid. She was right. Without any warning whatsoever, my arm was firmly in her grip. I had been through the drill before. It was time to shake her off and run. This time, it didn't work. This policewoman had the grip of a Sumo wrestler. She took me to her precinct police station and was made to wait in a secure room. There was no way out. Not long after, I found myself whisked away and into a large white van. I suspected that I was being taken to another orphanage. I experienced the worst orphanage I could ever imagine and the best. I wondered what the next one would be like.

When we arrived, I could not believe what I saw. This place was massive! It was the largest orphanage in Korea, housing some 3,500 children and run by the

Catholic Church. After being checked for lice, my hair was shaved completely off. I was then placed in a small group of a couple of other boys. The nuns were the ones in charge and they ran a tight ship. There was no nonsense. They started to debrief me, first with my name, but that is the only thing that I was able to answer. Virtually every other question they asked, I could not answer. It's not that I didn't want to answer them, rather I truly could not.

This orphanage was basically a good place. While it was not as free flowing as the last one, it was clean and safe, a far cry from the house of horrors I experienced at one time. I did settle into a daily routine. In a measured way, some of the joy that comes from being in a secure and safe place returned. After a couple of months though, my initial mission to find my parents began to work deep inside my spirit once more. Like all of the other orphanages in my past, it was now my plan to run away.

To my young and invincible mind, there was no place that could hold me. After carefully looking things over, I could not use the old escape template to which I had grown accustomed. Unlike the very lax environments of previous orphanages, this one employed some unusual measures. For starters, there was a twenty-five foot wall. Secondly, ominous looking barbed wire was coiled at the very top. I wondered if that was to keep people out or to keep us in. As unscalable as that wall looked, I knew that I could make my way out.

When the day came that I decided to make my escape, like before, I hid well as all of the children scurried around getting ready for morning classes. So far, so good. As the courtyard emptied and all of the students were securely in their classrooms, I made my move. I ran toward the wall where there were boxes stacked up against it. Using the boxes gave me the boost I needed to reach the top of the wall. Despite the noise of scaling the boxes, I remained unnoticed. After reaching the top, I jumped on top of the barbed wire to swing to the other side. My focus was so intent on the escape, I had not noticed how painful scraping against the barbed wire was. With my hands now grasping the other side of the barbed wire, I moved side to side to begin lowering myself. I saw that the wall was tapered. I thought this would help me slow down as I worked my way down the wall, but I overestimated my ability to control the descent. As my hands and arms grew weak, I was unable to hold on to the top any longer. I let go and began tumbling down to the ground, twenty-five feet below. I landed on my posterior and somehow hit my forehead on the ground in the process. Blood began to gush profusely from the injury I sustained to my forehead. Dazed, I just sat there for a moment wondering what I should do.

Someone saw what happened and immediately called security. In less than a minute, people surrounded me in compassion, scooped me up and starting attending to my injuries. Fortunately, they were able to stop the bleeding. Upon closer examination, everyone was amazed that I was not injured beyond the laceration on my forehead. There were no broken bones. How was that possible after falling from such a great height? There was no mistaking that God had dispatched angels to cushion the fall. It was yet another miracle.

The people in charge of the orphanage were not angry with my escape attempt. Instead, they were befuddled. Not a single child under their care had ever felt the need to escape. They could not take the chance that I would try this again anytime soon, so I was locked up in a tall building with very tight security. Like other parts of the orphanage, there were a lot of kids but many more staffers to keep order.

There were bunk beds in every room, stacked three high. Not having complete control over my bladder at night, there were mornings that I woke wet in a puddle of my own urine. I was punished every time this happened, being made to walk back and forth on my knees in the hallway with my hands over my head while the other children watched and laughed. I'm sure that they were trying to help me, but I also knew that this punishment would not solve the issue.

There were some pleasant aspects of life here, though. I remember being allowed outside to play soccer every once in a while. I also remember that our meals were brought up by elevator. On American Thanksgiving Day, turkey was brought up for dinner. One large piece of turkey was given to every three kids to split. We loved the taste so much that we wasted nothing. We even ate the bones!

Religious studies were mandatory. Religion was taught by the nuns. It was a part of our daily routine. In the evening, we watched Bible lesson movies and were taught how to pray. One of the prayers was the "Hail, Mary." I didn't get why we had to kneel and pray to Mary, but I just did what was expected of me. I truly had no desire to get into anymore trouble. I did, however, like my rosary beads. It's not that they helped me pray any better, rather, it had a cross on the end of it that glowed in the dark. Because I was afraid of the dark, that little glowing cross brought me an unspeakable comfort. There were countless nights where it would help me to fall asleep.

With so much American influence in this place, I began to long for a land I never knew existed. Korea was my world for seven years. Was there really a world outside Korea? Apparently so. There were many television shows that we were allowed to watch, many of them portraying life in America. On numerous occasions, we would sit around a daydream about one day living in America. Then one day, I announced to everyone I could that I was going to America. It wasn't a matter of if, but when. Most of them just laughed at me. That did not dampen a dream that was birthed that day in my heart. I was going to America and I knew in my heart that God chose me to go there at seven years old. That did not happen immediately. While I waited, by faith, a saw myself heading for the United States of America and spoke those words as if it were a done deal.

The Bible says: As it is written: "I have made you a father of many nations." He is our father in the sight of God, in whom he believed—the God who gives life to the dead and calls into being things that were not." (Romans 4:17 NIV). It had not yet happened, but I called my move to America as a fait accompli.

# Chapter 5:
# Going To America

Life in the Catholic orphanage eventually became the new normal. While I still thought about my parents and still had it in my heart to find them someday, it slowly moved out of the center of why I was living. My new vision of moving to America moved into the middle of the purpose for my existence. After being ridiculed for announcing to my friends and classmates that I was, in no uncertain terms, going there someday, I kept that dream close to the vest. I thought about it frequently during my day, but I did not talk about it like I did before. I did as I was told, and I tried to blend into the bigger picture. It made my young life, and the orphanage managers' lives, much less stressful. Instead of always trying to swim against the tide, I made a conscious decision to go with the flow.

One day, that flow was disrupted. Unlike the other episodes, I was not the source of it this time. It caught me off guard. I was being pulled out of class and told that someone in the main office needed to tell me something. Many things were racing in my mind. What did I do? Was there someone angry with me? Am I being punished for something, something I did not do? Could it actually be something good?

I was escorted into one of the nice offices where I was introduced to a lady from America. Her smile immediately diffused any thought that I was in trouble. Everyone around me seemed very pleasant and in a very good mood. Then there were photos. The lady from America was taking a ton of photos from every angle imaginable. I could not help wondering why she was taking so many photos. Then she stopped and spoke in a very strange language to the man in charge of the office. After a few minutes, the manager turned to me and gave me the news that I knew I would someday hear.

"Jon, you are being adopted by an American couple. You will soon be flying to your new home in America!"

While I knew that I would one day hear this, I had great difficulty believing that this was actually happening. Going to America was no longer a dream. It was time to get ready to leave. I was given a bag of wonderful presents from my new family in America. They were not in Korea, but the lady that was in the office was somehow responsible for bringing me back. It felt as though I was in the process of being born again. I had a chance to a new, better life. While I did think of my parents, this time it was only in passing. I realized that too much time had passed since we were separated, and that finding them now seemed impossible. In my mind, I officially suspended my search for them, but only for now. Perhaps someday I would return and have better success at trying to locate them.  As best as I could, I sealed up every good memory that I had of them and carefully placed them in a very deep nook in my heart.  I wanted to keep these special memories alive in my heart as I traveled to America.

Once the office visit was over, I was taken back upstairs to my classmates and friends.  I was bursting at the seams to tell them the great news.  I was going to America, just like I told them!  Many of them were genuinely very happy that my big break in life had finally arrived.  A few of them were jealous.  While I did not understand that very well then, I certainly do now.

The next 24 hours was a blur.  There was so much to do to prepare for my departure the next day.  I had a great deal of help packing, although admittedly, I did not have many belongings to pack.  It was then that I found out that another girl was coming to America with me as well and being adopted by another American family.  We were both so excited as we put our belongings into a van that drove us to the airport.

Up to that point, I had never seen a big airport much less been inside a terminal.  I was overwhelmed by the throngs of people going to and fro with suitcases and bags.  They all had far more belongings than me!  I wondered why they were all traveling with everything that they owned, or though it seemed.  Then I saw the jets.  They were larger than I could comprehend.  How can these giant things fly?  I was about to find out.

When I boarded with my friend, I was given the window seat. I wasted no time in drinking in all the activity outside the aircraft on the tarmac. When everyone was seated and all of the luggage was stored in the aircraft's belly, we began to taxi down to the runway. My heart was racing from the excitement. Then we took off. The feeling from rising into the air was beyond description. Just when I thought I was seeing the best part of the flight, something better happened. We popped through the clouds and were now on top of them instead of below them. It was amazing.

I stared out the window without boredom for hours on end. How often does a Korean orphan my age ever get to see such things? Eventually, flying over the ocean became monotonous, and the adrenalin of flying to a new country and to my new family wore out. I drifted off from time to time until I heard that the American shoreline was approaching. My adrenalin began to flow again. I was wide awake with anticipation. Suddenly, there it was! America. After we landed, I was escorted off of that plane and on to another one. My trip was not yet finished.

The last leg of my journey was relatively brief considering how long it took to reach America from Korea. This place called America is surely a very far away land. Despite that daunting thought, not once did I regret leaving Korea behind for now.

Upon arriving, my new family was excitedly waiting for me in the lobby. My adoptive mother, sisters and brother wore big, friendly smiles as they tried to make me feel welcomed into their world. I would meet my adoptive father a little later. We tried to greet each other the best we could, but I did not understand the language at all. I wasn't too concerned about that. I knew that, in time, I would begin to speak and understand more and more English. In the meantime, it was a little frustrating. Nonetheless, in their kindness, they brought an English-Korean dictionary so that they could begin to communicate with me.

# Chapter 6:
# Growing Up American

In an effort to keep the grand spotlight focused on our new, happy family, the lady who accompanied me and the other little girl to America unceremoniously bade us farewell. The girl met her new family at the airport, too. All too quickly, they faded down the concourse and out of sight. I wondered if our paths would ever cross again. That thought was only fleeting since something bigger than what I could put my arms around was happening. I was quickly being scooped up, hugged and loved by my new family members. The expressions of love were beyond description. I was truly happy for the very first time since my parents abandoned me in Korea.

Because it was late, we went to a local hotel to get some rest since the drive to my new home would be a long one. Even though it was a short drive, my body was not accustomed to auto motion in America and I threw up in the car. I wondered if my new family would not love me as much but there wasn't a shred of evidence that my motion sickness would change their mind about me.

We reached the hotel and we were all so happy together. I remember not being able to contain my joy. One of the only ways I could express that joy and happiness was to jump on the bed like a trampoline. One of my jumps was just a little too aggressive. I lost my balance and careened into the wall. I remember seeing what looked like stars and fireflies dancing around me. Everyone surrounded me to see if I was OK. My new mother sat down with me to settle me down.

She turned on the television and it was exciting to see real American television in real time. There was only one problem. I did not understand a word of what they were saying. Unlike the Korean audio dubs that were woven into the American television shows in Korea, there was no need for them here. I wondered if I would ever understand what they were saying. That's when my new family broke out their translation book and tried to communicate with me in my own native tongue. They were showing how genuine their love was for me. That needed no translation. I knew that I was in good hands and that I was safe and loved. That's all I needed to know to eventually fall into a deep and relaxing sleep that night.

When morning arrived, I felt refreshed and energized. It was almost an odd sensation since most of the time, even at the orphanage, sleep was almost always restless. While I lived on the street, sleep was a luxury and I grabbed it in small chunks when I thought it would be safe enough to do.

It was time to drive to my new home. The drive was long. I had to wait many hours to see my new home and meet my entire family. When we finally arrived, I continued to be overwhelmed with gratitude as I met my adopting father. Three things immediately struck me about him. He was tall, bald and bearded. That might be a rather intimidating combination if he had not looked at me and smiled a smile that was warm and inviting. I had no trouble calling him "Dad" immediately.

A chow dog came to greet me with its dog smile as well. I felt like an international celebrity when the neighbors began coming over to welcome me to the neighborhood. It was a great feeling.

Dad's work on the midnight shift was very demanding, but Mom made it work since she worked at the local hospital in the daytime. Mom had one daughter by an earlier marriage, but very early in their marriage, her husband died from a rare blood disorder while he was only in his twenties. Mom eventually remarried the man I came to know as my Dad. Because he had constant exposure to certain warfare chemicals during his tour of duty in the Vietnam War, he could not have children. They chose to adopt three children. One of them was from America and two were from South Korea, one of whom was me. The more I got to know my new family, the more I loved them. There was plenty of joy all around us.

Shortly after I was settled with my new family, it was time to become a United States citizen. It was so exciting to travel to downtown Canton, Ohio at the

Civic Center. I remember having to raise my right hand and having to repeat an oath. I repeated in the best English that I could. Apparently, it was good enough. I was now a citizen of the United States of America! We celebrated my new citizenship by eating at the iconic American eatery, McDonald's. It was my first time there. My meal tasted so delicious!

I had to pinch myself. Was this all a wonderful dream from which I would wake, or was this really happening to me? It felt like it was only moments ago when I was temporarily resigned to living life in an orphanage in a monotonous daily routine. Now I had my loving American parents surrounding me with love, a beautiful home, complete with siblings, aunts, uncles, grandparents, nieces, and nephews! It was wonderful. I did not, however, forget that somewhere in Korea, I had a birth mother and a father that were somewhere. I couldn't help thinking that they would be surprised, maybe even sad, that I was now living halfway around the world. Perhaps someday I would have the opportunity to resume my search for them in Korea. I tucked that thought in a safe nook in my heart and got to the business of learning the American way of life.

When it was time to enroll me in school, I naturally had some reservations and insecurities. Everything was going great up to that point. I was starting to learn the language and beginning to operate reasonably well in the American culture. Nonetheless, the thought of school made me nervous. My classmates were all about my size, but they were all so uniformly different from me.

My fear was truly unfounded. I quickly realized that they were doing everything possible to embrace me unconditionally. Making friends was far easier than I thought it would be, even with my struggle to learn English. Watching wonderful programs like Sesame Street and Mister Rogers' Neighborhood helped to speed my transition from Korean to English and I was assigned a speech teacher who also helped me in my journey to communicate in this new language. Within a short period of time, I was able to write and speak in English, but somehow I knew that I had an accent that I could not shed. I was especially self conscious about my accent when called upon to read out loud to the class. I simply hated my accent.

Despite my new challenges, I was determined to do my best and to try to fit in as best as I could. My determination must have been the key to my dramatic improvement in every area of school life, from academic to social pursuits. My academic advances were so rapid, that the teachers moved me up in my classes during the year. It also helped that, both in and out of the classroom, my teachers and classmates seemed to like me. This set me at ease. I started to laugh and joke with my classmates. I remember getting the biggest kick out of gently squeezing the cheeks of my classmates, many insisting that they would be next. I had this innocent fascination with softness and my classmates thought it was funny and entertaining.

This group was also responsible for getting me into the YMCA to play basketball, swim, and play soccer. In the summer, the YMCA would open up the pool to the public. It was always busy and a great place to hang out to meet new people. Add activities as a new Boy Scout and there was no room for boredom. I also joined one of the local Little League Baseball teams for our school. I remember enjoying the camaraderie, but also remember that I truly wasn't someone that had a talent to play baseball.

Despite the gains I had made in so many areas, there was a new challenge that developed when I was in the fourth grade. My vision began to become blurry. So many things started to become out of focus. My parents, recognizing that I was having an issue, took me to the eye doctor who confirmed that I needed glasses. Even decades ago, eyeglasses were not inexpensive and not covered by insurance back then. Regardless, my parents purchased a pair of subscription eyeglasses for me. It was great to be able to see again, but I was still a boy who did not understand that I needed to treat my new eyewear with caution and care. They broke more than once and I had to be content with makeshift fixes.

Once grade school was behind me, I moved to Faircrest Middle School located just south of downtown Canton. My favorite class was art because I loved to draw and I was actually very good at it. I will forever remember the encouragement that the art teacher gave me. She told me that I had a real talent and encouraged me to keep at it. Finally, something that I was very, very good at! I knew that she wasn't just feeding me a line because I entered and won a school yearbook contest that required students to submit a drawing. Mine was of the school with two eagles poised on each side of the building. What a great feeling to know that I was the best at something. I was able to add one more item to that category by the end of middle school as well. I also had the record for the most pull-ups in the entire school up to that point. I was on a roll. From that point on, the school seasons went by quickly. I became popular with both students and teachers and had a large company of good friends.

Up to the time I was nine, my spiritual development was developed by my life experience. I knew that I had "Someone" who was watching over me. Who wouldn't at least suspect that after seeing so many rescues from bad situations that should have meant the end of my earthly life? But that was the extent of it until I received an invitation to attend a church camp. It sounded like lots of fun. Always enjoying a new adventure, I jumped at the chance. Having many others my age who practiced kindness was something I took special note of. I also sensed that my camp group leader really cared about me. He was simply expressing the love of Christ, whom he served. All the camp leaders, given the chance, showed their genuine interest in each camper as they told us about the love of God through His Son, Jesus. I loved hearing about Someone that sounded so familiar and close. I felt as though I was being introduced to the Higher Power who was watching over me when I was a street kid in Korea.

One evening, a camp-wide event was planned. As we gathered together, there was signing. People got up and told their personal stories of how they met Jesus Christ. They called them testimonies. At the end, the pastor asked if there was anyone who had not yet met Jesus and wanted to invite Him as their personal Savior. Something deep inside me was stirring. I knew that the only way to quell the feeling was to raise my hand, even though I was not completely sure what I was doing. I just knew that I needed to receive the One who was watching over me since I was born. The pastor made the choice so plain and so simple. It was exactly what I wanted. The salvation and the love of Jesus. Looking back at that special evening, it was the best decision that I have ever made.

The minute someone invites Jesus into their heart, eternal salvation is certain. But the process of becoming more Christ-like is a lifelong journey on this side of eternity. There was no better example of that than me. Even after such a heartwarming conversion, I still managed to get myself into a lot of trouble as I was growing up.

Here's an example. My brother and I once found some spray paint. We ran over to the schoolyard teeter-totter where I giggled as I spray painted my name on it. By virtue of the act, I was advertising who it was that just vandalized school property. Yet when the principal later asked me if I knew who it was who spray-painted the teeter-totter, I told him that I did not know. But even early in my walk with the Lord, the Holy Spirit convicted my heart that I had not only done something wrong, but that I lied about it. Not being able to stand the feeling of guilt, I went back and told him that it was me.

There was another time that my brother and I rode out to the dump. We liked riding our bikes there because there were lots of dirt hills and ramps that we used as if we were on an obstacle course. This one particular time, my brother convinced me to try smoking pine needles inside of a rolled newspaper. I can still remember how nasty it was. Then he pulled out a handful of almost-spent cigarettes from our father's ash tray at home to smoke. I hacked my lungs out. It was my first cigarette and it was my last one, too.

As I began to mature, feelings of abandonment began to creep in and I started becoming depressed, and even angry at times. My hope of ever reuniting with my birth parents in Korea was lost. I gave up on them. I thought that I might still have an ember of love remaining somewhere in my heart, but there were days when I wondered if that ember was still glowing. Up to that point, I was a pretty happy child no matter what my circumstances were. Why were these feelings now starting to bubble up? Little did I know that this was only the beginning of a turbulent period in my life. Major trouble lie ahead, not only for me, but for all of my family members.

# Chapter 7:
# Family Facade

Up until now, my time in America was like a storybook fairy tale. Despite the challenges of trying to mesh into a new culture and a new language, life was very good. The honeymoon period was now over. Many unsettling feelings that I never knew existed were now haunting me. We were all now so comfortable with one another as a family that we started seeing the real people emerge. I found it interesting that you start to really see people with much more clarity after you get to know them well.

Here's a little about my siblings. I have two sisters and one brother. My oldest sister was the birth child of my adopted mother. The other two were adopted. My younger sister was adopted as a baby from Korea. My older brother was adopted from inside the United States. It surely sounded like a juvenile mish mash, potentially a recipe of all kinds of mischief. But I believe that the root of the family turbulence that we were about to enter stemmed first from our parents.

On the outside, we appeared to be a normal, church-going family who went to a church in Massillon, Ohio virtually every Sunday. On the inside, there were a number of secret sins lurking in the darkness. My brother and I stumbled across some startling items in my parent's bedroom, for instance. Pornographic magazines were stashed away neatly in my father's sock drawer. I then learned about the pornographic world from my brother. I was only ten or eleven years old when he explained things to me that should have been reserved for my parents to tell me as I grew mature enough to understand about such things.

In hindsight, I would have to say that my brother enjoyed his vices and bad habits and tried to get me to join him in many of his escapades, such as smoking cigarettes and pot. Many of the artifacts from those escapades are something for which I was singled-out and constantly blamed for. My parents never caught on to the fact that it was my brother who was the one involved in so many questionable activities. He was clearly headed for trouble. Trouble arrived in a big way as the years rolled by. His drinking increased to the point of landing him a DUI. Only temporarily was he frightened when he sought help from his drug and alcohol dependence, but the motivation to change his direction was short-lived. When he was old enough, he packed his bags and left for Alaska. We never heard from him again.

My older sister was nowhere near the headache as my brother, but she was still your typical rival sibling. I think she liked being mean to me. She hardly ever spoke to me or appreciated my presence. Like my brother, she smoked and drank as well, but it was not at the same level as my brother. Still, she was unstable enough to try to commit suicide at age fourteen by a pill overdose of some sort. Fortunately, she was found and rushed to the hospital in time to save her life. Unfortunately, she became pregnant at age seventeen. She married the father of the unborn child. Soon after, we went in different directions and it was the last time we've ever been in contact.

As I mentioned before, my father was somewhat of a mystery to me for many reasons. He worked at night and slept during the day, so I did not have the opportunity to develop that father-son bond that I was hoping for. However, I did learn some things about him that helped me to understand his dark world. After serving our country in Vietnam, he returned with problems. Some may even call what he had PTSD. Because of his constant exposure to the defoliant called agent orange, he was not able to have any children of his own. While he did not speak often about some of the specifics of his tour of duty, he did tell a story once about a commander that ordered him to shoot and kill a group of kids that were a lot like me when I was young. The reason behind the order was that they did not want these kids to have the chance to kill U.S. soldiers. He believed that by adopting kids from Korea, he could make amends for the lives that he was ordered to end. That story began to reveal the reason why my father was such a distant and quiet man.

There were other moments that were just plain strange. Once, we "camped out" in the basement on the couch-bed that was there. He took off everything except his underwear and told my brother and I to do the same. Nothing else happened at all. We just all sat there, silent and uncomfortable, for what seemed like the longest time. To this day, I have no idea what that was all about.

The relationship that he had with my mother was cool at best. They did not seem to be close. I never really saw them hug or kiss each other very much like I used to see depicted on American television. For every time I saw them hug or kiss, I must have witnessed dozens of fights where they would scream and yell at each other. This was sadly the norm in our house. It went on for years. In my teenage mind, I simply could not understand how they ever became man and wife. Even though I have not heard from either of them for over twenty years, I do know that they eventually divorced.

When I initially came to the United States and joined my new family, my mother was okay. But as time wore on, she became bitter and angry towards me in particular. What I had dreamed about in that Korean orphanage never really came to pass. I wanted, so badly, the unconditional love of a mother. It became increasingly clear that she was not going to fulfill that desire.

The one of the hardest time period for me to navigate through the storms of family discouragement was between the ages of nine and eleven. I simply could not process why my mother seemed to love every one of her children except for me. At every turn, I was the object of something that was done or said that was mean in every sense of the word. Where was kindness? Where was compassion? Where was caring? Where was love? Instead, I was continually bombarded with disparaging words and told that I wasn't any good and that I was not a good son. At one point, I could not take it anymore and told my mother that I wanted to go back to Korea. At least the people in the last orphanage in which I lived were not mean. My mother then tried to convinced me that if I went back to Korea that everyone there would hate me and spit on me. I seemed to have no where to turn.

Several other episodes come to mind during this period. I remember having to bite off a piece of soap after using foul language just before leaving for school. I held that piece of soap in my mouth even after walking into my classroom. The teacher noticed that there was something wrong with me. At this point, my mouth was burning and ulcerated. The teacher had compassion and sent me to the bathroom to rinse out my mouth.

Do you remember how I told you that I used to get a kick out of gently squeezing other people's cheeks? Somehow, my mother found this out and proceeded to tell me that my doing so was an act of cruelty to others. Then she came over and squeezed my cheeks with her powerful adult fingers as hard as she could for what seemed like an eternity. My eyes teared up, not from the sadness of being humiliated but from the pain of my cheeks being squeezed. I'm sure that I had an imprint from her vice-like grip for days.

Sadly, this was my "normal," my world.

There were times when I was at the end of my rope. By this time, I was twelve years old. Being a pre-pubescent twelve year old boy all by itself is a difficult time for any kid to navigate. Add all of the other heartache and family trouble and you may understand why life started looking so hopeless to me. I began to question if life was worth living anymore. I spiraled into a deep depression and it seemed like no one could help. In my mind, happiness is something that I would never find. Absolutely nothing made me feel better. I hated everything around me. I did not care about anything anymore. I was cursed to live this awful life that had been dealt to me.

Trying to numb the pain of my existence in any way that I could occupied much of my time. I picked up the habit of smoking cigarettes. When I could find it, I smoked pot. It helped to numb the emotional pain, but I was always disappointed with how temporary the relief was. I tried some very unusual things such as inhaling gasoline fumes and freon to get high. Along with all of that came the heavy metal music. I knew full well that my pathway was a destructive one, but I truly did not care. Deep inside, I hoped that my miserable existence would simply end. In hindsight, all of these actions and thoughts were from the pit of hell and the devil himself, but it wasn't happening fast enough.

One evening, I laid out plans to kill myself. I sat down and began thinking about the quickest and easiest way to end my life. I entertained using knives, fire, and water as instruments of death. Then I remembered all of the medicines that my parents took for their health problems.

That evening, I waited until everyone was gone from the house. As soon as I was sure that I had the whole house to myself, I took all of the medicine bottles out of the cupboard and poured them all out on the table. There must have been hundreds of pills of varying sizes and colors covering the table. I stared at the pills on the table for an hour. Was there any reason not to do this? I couldn't think of a single one. I bought the devil's lie. I grabbed a handful of the pills, filled my mouth and began swallowing them with the help of a glass of water. The feeling of all of those pills going down to my stomach was awful. It was as if I tried swallowing a handful of gravel. I took another handful and did it again, and again, and again, until there were no more pills to swallow. Then I waited.

At first, nothing happened. Several hours passed and I still felt nothing happening. Many hours after sunset, deep in the night, I started to feel sick.

That's when my mother came home from work. I started feeling much worse and decided to tell my mother what I had done. At first it was as if she did not believe me, but panic suddenly came over her when she realized that I was not faking how badly I was feeling. She told me to get into the car. It was at that point that I could no longer walk and simply fell over. My brother was now home and he had to carry me to the car for our drive to the hospital. By the time we reached the hospital, I was crying from the pain I was in, especially my head.

The doctors rushed me in and made me drink a horrible charcoal antidote, but it was little use since so many of the drugs had already started assimilating into my bloodstream and attacking my organs. Nothing they did was helping me. I was dying. Somehow I remember my father coming to the hospital. He was weeping over me and asking why I had done such a thing. Then I remembered nothing.

The doctors actually pronounced me dead after several minutes without a pulse. Fortunately, their attempts to revive me were successful. After several hours, they flew me to the major children's hospital in the city where emergency surgery was waiting for me. In order to save my life, they had to drain the fluid around my heart. There was one very big problem. I had so many different kinds of medicine inside my body that I could not be given any anesthesia. Drilling a hole in my chest to insert a tube woke me out of my drug-induced sleep. The pain of the procedure was almost too much to bear. I cried the whole time. A very compassionate nurse stood by my side and held my hand to offer distraction and comfort.

After what seemed like a very long time, the doctors were done and they were confident that my life had been spared. I was given a very big second chance. Despite my depression, I sensed that God did care and wanted me to live. It was the hope I needed to press on in this life's journey.

My recovery took all of three months. Upon realizing that it was time to go home, I cringed at the thought of having to face everyone in my family. Part of the continuing home recovery was counseling. It did very little to get rid of my intense feeling that I did not want to be in my parent's home anymore. Being there thrust me right back into depression and fear. Once again, I wanted to die. Counseling actually made things worse since I was forced to have to spend time around a mother that I felt really disliked me.

My case worker suggested another course of action. They sent me to a place where others my age went to recover from depression and other similar problems. It was like going camping, so it was better than being at home. After being there a while, it was time to go back home. The therapist to whom I was assigned put me on an antidepressant to help me to cope with the way I felt about life in general. All that did was put me in a kind of daze, only blurring the emotional pain I had. With little sense of self-esteem or of being loved, I was in and out of the hospital's suicide ward for teens for many months. The devil had a firm grip on me, encouraging me to focus on everything negative from anxiety, depression, anger, and fear.

I began dealing with the fear of my mother in a variety of ways. The easiest was simply to make myself as scarce as possible. When she arrived home from work in the evening, I would quietly hide in my room. That seemed to work as best as it could since my father did nothing to help me. He seemed to live in the background and had no desire to get involved. In time, however, the way in which I dealt with her started to change, mainly because I was growing up. I was getting bigger in size. I realized that I could now physically defend myself if I had to. The taller I grew, the less she frightened me. I could now fight back.

To this day, I try to make sense of why she suddenly became so abusive to me. Did she have other problems that made her cranky? Did she take things out on me because I was the easy target in our family? Was she abused herself as a child? Even if she was, it was no excuse to be so mean to me. Couldn't she see what she was doing to me? There were many scars over the years, some physical and many more emotional. The result? I was building a wall around me. I built that emotional wall so that she could not hurt me anymore. The unintended consequence was that I lived my life in increasing isolation.

Those painful days were about to end, accelerated by yet another explosive event while driving home from church one Sunday. From the passenger side of the car, my mother was once again criticizing me for something. Our words became heated. I could not take the abuse anymore. I blew up in her face and punched her as hard as I could. She was in shock. Thank goodness my father had to pay attention to his driving. Had he not been driving, I fear for what he would have done to me in the heat of the moment. After we arrived home, he did not do anything, but I sensed that our relationship had changed from one of total indifference to one of anger and resentment.

From that point on, I was fearful for my life. It was then that I called Children Services and told them as much as I could in a nutshell. The response was almost immediate. After quickly assessing the situation, they removed me from their home for my own safety. It was the last time that I ever had to live with them. I was amazed that someone actually believed me and wanted to do something to protect me.

I still struggle wondering why I had to do through all of that. The inviting and normal looking house on the outside was nothing but a facade. It was a house of pain and suffering. Nonetheless, I forgave my adoptive parents long ago. I hold nothing against them at all. I did this in obedience according to the Words of my Lord, Jesus. It's my obligation to extend grace to others since Jesus offered me the ultimate grace that brought me from death to eternal life.

# Chapter 8:
# Meeting The Wilsons

It's truly amazing at how a person's surroundings can influence a soul's well-being. After being removed from that toxic family environment, and placed into a loving family home, the signs of my depression began to disappear. That loving family home was that of the Wilsons. I immediately felt their love and compassion as they welcomed me into their home. If only this was the family that would have been my first American home when I arrived from Korea.

The Wilsons received me with tender loving care, just as they had done for many years for other foster kids that came through the Wilson's home for temporary placement. Our bonding was fast and genuine. They loved me unconditionally for who I was. There was another boy there for a little while. He was from Vietnam and did not speak any English. His stay with the Wilsons was much shorter as he was sent back to his own country.

It was here, at the Wilson's home, that I saw how a family was supposed to look. They had five natural children. As unique as each of their own children were, each one of them was loved and cared for equally, with no sign of favoritism. We ate together in peace. We watched movies together and laughed. I felt as though I was living in a dream that was far too good to be true.

One of the family meals that I enjoyed most was something the Wilsons called cabbage and noodles. It quickly became my very favorite when we came together to the table. It consisted of homemade noodles, cabbage, chicken, corn, mushrooms, and seasonings. It may not sound like much, but to me, the combination was heavenly. It was made even better when we shared it all together as a fun-loving family.

My time there was truly too short. Because they were a foster family, the kids they welcomed were often moved to other locations only months after they arrived. Such was the case with me. Three months after I arrived, I was told that it was time to say goodbye. They gave me the love that almost faded from my memory, the kind that I remembered as a distant memory from my parents when I was a toddler in Korea, the kind I yearned for and finally found in the Wilson home. When the time came to say our goodbyes, we all cried, but they promised to stay in touch with me. That promise was not just lip service. They meant it, and they did, in fact, follow through and stayed in touch with me as they were able.

I then spent time in a detention center to wait for a more permanent arrangement, or even a solution to reunite me to my first American family, something I hoped would not happen.

During my time at the detention center, I got to know many of the other kids that were there. Most of the time, they were there because of some serious trouble they got into, and were removed from their parent's home. As I got to know them, all of them did not seem to be the kinds of kids that got into deep trouble. One of the common denominators, however, was a bad childhood environment. Having no choice in that, many of them simply acted out of frustration.

Life in the center was somewhat boring, so I busied myself by lifting weights in the gym. I spent hours every day there. Soon, my body started showing it, and I was pleased with seeing physical dividends paying off. Despite the new focus, the place was still a detention center. The doors were always locked to prevent anyone of us from leaving.

There were periods when things operated less like a detention center and more like a kid's camp. At times, we were allowed to go outside to play sports. There were other times when we would take group trips to Cedar Point, or to other Ohio parks to explore together. School was something that the center made sure was solid. The schedule was reliable and serious. Most of the time, the boys and the girls were separated, but every once in awhile, we had an activity that was co-ed when it was appropriate, however, we were all watched so closely that no one had any thought of doing anything that would halt that privilege.

The center's housing, however, was not uniform. The kids that were easier to handle, like me, stayed in a cottage. Those that misbehaved constantly were kept in an intimidating building where the security was very tight. Most of the kids eventually returned to their families after their behavior seemed stable and respectful. Unfortunately, there were a few that continued to be combative. In hindsight, it was this group that, by and large, would eventually find themselves locked up in prison for serious crimes.

Only three months after arriving there, I was approved for moving into a group home.

# Chapter 9:
# Group Home And Counseling

I lived in a group home from the time I was fourteen years old until I was eighteen, about four years. The environment was not as intimidating. There were a total of nine kids living in the group home I was in. The staff cooked all the meals and arranged all the daily activities. I remember that free milk was delivered to us every week, but we could not consume it fast enough. Sometimes, we threw out gallons of milk because it went past the expiration date.

Most of my housemates were there for minor situations. Most of them were sent back home after behaving well. I had to share a bedroom with three other boys. That part was easy. The part that wasn't was the odor of the room. One of the boys wet his bed virtually every morning. Our bedroom's urine stench was difficult to take. I felt bad for the boy since his issue seemed to be medical.

I was not immune from physical issues. The polio I had meant that I could not run well. My right leg muscles were not as strong as my left. It seemed like each one of us had something unique to deal with. This made our time outside playing sports awkward for me. Because we all had unique quirks, it's understandable that we would occasionally get pulled into minor fights, but they didn't last long and we were able to shake hands and move on.

While we were allowed to leave during the day, there was a hard curfew that everyone respected. But during the non-curfew period, many of the boys in the group home left to spend time with their girlfriends. In a way, I was a bit envious. I felt alone. This only fueled my depression and often pushed me to entertain suicidal thoughts. Deep inside my heart, I was mad and angry. In hindsight, I now see that my low self-esteem was the platform from which anger would erupt toward others around me.

I can't count the number of times during which I entertained thought of ending my life. That usually happened at night when I was alone with my own thoughts. I recognized that I was perpetually unhappy and downright miserable. No matter what I did, I could not seem to get better. At one point, my anger toward God manifested itself when I took a nearby Bible and ripped out all the pages. After I was done, I cut my wrist in an attempt to end my suffering. Someone discovered what I had done and I was rushed to the hospital where I spent weeks healing. Thankfully, the cut was not deep enough.

Overall, the staff at the group home did what they could to provide us with some structure and stability. There was a morning staff, an evening staff, and an overnight staff. Most of them were very nice, but there was one staffer that seemed to really care about me and everyone there. It made sense when I discovered that he was a Christian. His love for us was apparent. It's a shame that someone like that wasn't my licensed counselor. I had to go see one every week. We did talk about how to be calm and to think positive thoughts. He also put me on an antidepressant which did seem to help a little.

In the end, counseling didn't help because I had a wall around the "real me." I wouldn't let anyone near that wall. Every time I believed one of them was getting just a little too close to that "real me," I immediately went into defense mode and would not allow anyone to come close.

One time, one of the kids in the group home invited me to go to church with his Aunt and Uncle. Something about it sounded attractive, so I accepted his invitation. I was immediately enamored by all of the joyful people I saw everywhere! During the message, the Pastor gave an invitation to receive Christ and be saved. I knew that I had done that at the kid's camp, but I wanted to make sure that I was saved, so I went forward during the invitation. I loved the security and freedom I felt at church, so I a started going every Sunday. It didn't take long for people to want to get to know me better and to share their encouragement in the faith. Immediately, my "wall" came up. I no longer wanted to go to church. I told the family that was taking me that I no longer wanted to go to church with them on Sunday mornings. They did everything they could to talk me out of my sudden change of heart, but I saw their plea as an assault and I started to yell at them. They were getting too close to the "real me." If only I would have understood that their love for me was unconditional. They were simply trying to be my friend. It seemed like that cycle played out over and over again. I can't count the number of people who tried to help me, but I pushed away. I recognized how emotionally screwed up I was. I couldn't ever see myself getting better. It was at these moments that I felt hopeless.

Thankfully, there were brighter moments when I could forget about my emotional hurricane. Our group was occasionally treated to a day at Cedar Point, the local zoo, or to roller skate. We even had a week when we were take to a South Carolina beach! When I wasn't involved with one of those outings, I tried fitting in on the playground basketball court, and at other various sports venues. Christmas time was also one of those moments when I could forget about things. I remember seeing a treasure box full of Christmas gifts arrive from a local church. It made me temporarily feel good about life.

Too often, those highlights were too brief. During a normal school week, I was pulled back into horrible situations. All of us walked about a mile to and from school, but we all did not go to the same schools, so we did not walk together. A lot can happen in the space of a mile. One day, five other kids jumped me and tried to hurt me while I was on my way home. Fortunately, I was not seriously injured, but things like that made me even more angry and bitter. The result was that I did not have very many friends in school. It was not uncommon for me to be bullied.

I was once called terrible names by one boy. This enraged me to the point that I actually wanted to kill him. I went to school prepared for another altercation. Like I anticipated, the boy showed up and started hurling names my way. This time I was ready. I pulled out the scissors I had in my pocket and started waving it toward him. Fortunately for him, my aim was very bad. He withdrew and nothing serious happened until he went to the Principal's office and told him what I tried to do. Inevitably, I was called to the Principal's office. When he asked for the sharp object, I simply sat there, motionless, but enraged. I could feel the pressure building up like molten lava inside a volcano. After enough pressure had built up, I pulled out the scissors and tried to attack him. Alarmed, he called for help. Other teachers came, but all those teachers could not restrain me. Finally, someone called the police. It took four officers to restrain me. I was placed on a gurney and shuffled off to a psychiatric ward for a couple of weeks. The school from which I was removed never allowed me to return. All of this happened only weeks before I would have graduated and received my high school diploma. Now I was forced to finish my schooling in a place whose students were more out-of-control than me.

Once out of the hospital and back in the group home, I looked for opportunities to end my misery. I tried to commit suicide in every way imaginable. Nothing seemed to work. Only once was my attempt nearly successful when I cut my wrist and bled. The evening staff was making rounds when they saw what I had done. I was rushed to the hospital in time for doctors to save my life. Now, in hindsight, God was keeping me alive for a greater work and for His ultimate glory.

Through this tumultuous time, the Wilsons remained in contact with me. From time to time, I joined them for dinners and for Sunday church services. There were even times when I spent the night with them. There was something about them that allowed me to relax and not have to put up that near impenetrable wall around my heart and soul. The Wilson family was likely the only family that I felt comfortable enough to let them see into my broken soul. It was a place I let no one else go. As a result, we got to know each other on a level far deeper than I ever imagined possible.

# Chapter 10:
# College

I spent four years in the group home for boys until I turned eighteen. Once that happened, it was time to move out of the home. There weren't many choices for me at the time. The sudden shift from a semi-stable environment to yet another unknown was upsetting. Not knowing what to do, I simply accepted what was set up for me - college.

With eighty dollars a month for groceries and a dorm room, I was registered to take classes. About the only thing in my control was deciding what kind of degree to pursue. For years, I had to learn how to take care of myself when I was both well and when I was ill, sometimes very ill. The college's nursing program seemed like a good fit. Could it be that I found something in which I would thrive?

Once again, what little hope I had was quickly dashed. The courses associated with the nursing program were not only extremely hard, but I could not understand anything that my professors were saying. Some had unrecognizable accents. Others simply spoke too fast for someone whose primary language is Korean. Essentially, I was totally lost. Once again, the inferiority complex I struggled with erupted with renewed vigor. I left every class frustrated and angry.

When I looked around me, all I saw were kids that were so much better than me in every way.

I felt so alone. How in the world was I going to survive four long college years? Because the finances for the four-year degree program was taken care of, I felt completely trapped. Every negative thing that I thought I had put behind me started chasing after me and jumping on me. I can't really say that I made friends with anyone there. I started becoming emotionally unstable. My roommate and I never spoke to each other. We had absolutely nothing in common. I was a wreck and spiraling down back into the abyss with which I was all too familiar. After three weeks, I overdosed on my medication and was rushed to a hospital. That effectively ended my college career.

Once again, I was in a hospital recovering from an overdose. Imagine my surprise when two parties came to visit me. The first family that adopted me from Korea never showed up. Instead, the Wilsons and the Korean cobbler reached out to me. Each came to offer me a place to go after I was well enough to be released. The decision was pretty easy. As best as I could tell, the Korean cobbler's motivation was, at the very least, partially motivated by his shoe repair business. Once before, he helped me out by allowing me to stay in his apartment in exchange for assisting him in his business. While he did pay me, it was under the table and was minimal while the work day was long and very hard. Picturing this arrangement in my mind was horrifying.

All the while, every time I pictured myself with the Wilson family, I smiled.

# Chapter 11:
# Adoption At Eighteen

One might think that being embraced and loved by a family would cure every emotional ailment. That was at least the Wilson family's hope as they opened their home and their lives to me. How could anyone's life do better? The Wilsons took a step of faith that went far above and beyond offering me sone familial stability. They asked me if I would like to officially be adopted as a Wilson. When that day came, the entire Wilson family was at the courthouse. All of my soon-to-be brothers and sisters were there with warm smiles. I was getting adopted... at age eighteen! While everyone in their family, including me, was filled with joy and excitement, the rage that I buried for the moment was still hiding inside my spirit. I was a human ticking time bomb and the fuse was much shorter than anyone expected.

The sensation of "being a Wilson" was wonderful but very strange, too. I had truly never been a part of a close-knit family. Quite honestly, as much as I wanted to be in a family, I didn't really know how to act as a son, or as a brother. Perhaps it was the insecurity of not knowing how to "be a Wilson" that allowed my lingering spirit of rage a way to seep to the surface of who I had been, and was. These issues started off with small infractions and angry outbursts. But my new father and mother had been through this drill before.

The Wilsons had been host to a number of temporary foster children, many of whom were special needs kids. They had a special ministry and love for special needs kids and seemed to bring out the best of each over time. What other family would go out of their way to adopt a baby boy whose organs developed on the outside of his body because his birth mother was on drugs? The birth mother loved that baby, but realized that it was beyond her ability to care for the boy, so the Wilsons stepped in.

My new adopted family was loving and stable. My father worked hard at his day job so that my mother could be a stay-at-home caretaker for all of us. If there was any family that was going to weather the coming class five emotional hurricane, it was the Wilsons.

The anger that I had bottled up deep inside me began to emerge more and more often. The intensity of those outbursts also grew. Despite my emotional instability, the Wilsons possessed a preternatural and resolute force of love and patience. Even I could see that this kept them strong and committed to seeing me through my dark days. Sadly, I am ashamed to say that each day grew darker and darker. Not even knowing why I was acting with such cruelty, I pushed all of my family away, physically, mentally, and emotionally. I started fortifying that all-to-familiar wall of seclusion all around me.

They tried sending me to counseling. There was no improvement. I was put on an antidepressant. No effect. When my mother would try to engage me in casual conversation during her daily chores, she would do her best to try to add the kind of motherly love to help me, but that only stirred up the rage bubbling up from my spirit. Then there were times when I would simply express anger for no reason whatsoever. In hindsight, I had the ability to whip up my emotions into a feedback frenzy until I was out of control. The Wilsons weren't the ones making me mad. I could not allow myself to be happy. I was bitter, angry, unhappy, and highly unstable. I should have been enjoying happiness, joy, security, peace, and everything else that came along "being a Wilson," so on top of all of that emotional mess, I felt guilty for being surrounded by so much family love.

Mom's Christian faith drove her to her knees often for me. Her prayers for me must have arrived in heaven by the truckload. Other families would have given up on me long ago, but not the Wilsons. As many times as I pushed them away, they would open up their arms. Even though I was eighteen, I still had thoughts of "running away." There were many days when my parents couldn't find me around the house. Mom always knew where to find me. I can't count the number of times they found me at the local Greyhound bus station looking to escape, but to where? It's obvious to me now that while the spirit of God worked tirelessly through the Wilson family, the spirit that had control over me was the one at war with God.

At one point, I convinced my case worker to open up a spot for me at a group home, away from my adopted family's love and care. While my family was frustrated with their inability to break through my thick emotional walls, they were persistent and stayed in touch with me during this episode. I realize now that I was only running away from myself. The group home was filled with other individuals who were busy fighting their own demons. If they weren't there, they were spending lots of time in mental health clinics. None of them seemed to make any real progress while I was there. Despite many that came by to visit me, like an acquaintance from my family's church who talked to me about a gracious, loving God, and even my mother who said that I admitted to being controlled by Satan, I continued to be blinded by an irrational anger. Years later, my mother told me about that conversation and I was shocked. I never remembered saying such things! After a short time, I moved back home. Any improvement or progress I made was always temporary. It was no different back home.

Like before, my loving family never provoked me. In fact, they went above and beyond to give me the tools I needed for emotional health and stability. Their patience cut through the static of my own pent up anger. I noticed it, and even appreciated it, but only if I could do so at a safe distance. I watched as my pastor and my family surrounded me with prayer. They knew what they were up against. It wasn't a flesh and blood battle, but one taking place in the spiritual realm. Now, in hindsight, I shudder to think what would have happened if they didn't pray for me so passionately. What I didn't understand at the time is that everyone else saw that God had a divine purpose waiting for me.

Despite knowing full well that my adopted family loved me and was trying to help me to that new beginning, I was unwilling to let go of my cesspool of anger. It was almost as if I wanted to cling to it. Once again and without much warning, that cesspool explosively erupted one evening when a counselor had a session scheduled with me at the house. I can't even remember why I became so enraged, but in the heat of the moment, I slung a derogatory slur at my sister. She was well within her right to slap me, but her reason was not revenge. She slapped me to "wake me" out of my rant. Obviously, I didn't see it like that. Any restraint to my temper was totally gone. My reaction became so physical that my parents had to call the police.

You would have thought that their mere presence would have settled me down, but the exact opposite happened. The adrenalin rush made me impossible to restrain. I fought them until they collectively gained the upper hand. At the end of it all, I was under arrest, charged with domestic violence, and on my way to the Stark County jail, a place that became my "home" for a couple of months.

It's interesting how watching time go by confined by a jail cell forces anyone to spend that time thinking about the mess I was in. I had no one to blame but myself. From what I was later told, I was on suicide watch that first night. That meant I was naked and cold. There was nothing in that cell aside from a bed, mattress, and a toilet. On night one, staying warm was challenging. I had to bend the thin mattress around me in lieu of a blanket. When the guards saw that I would not be a threat to myself, I was allowed to watch television and even stretch my legs outside of the cell where I could talk to other people.

After a few months, I was released. My father picked me up and drove me home. I was so happy to be out of that place. The fresh air had a sweetness to it that, until that moment, I had always taken for granted.

The drive home was awkwardly quiet. Both of us didn't really know what to say to each other. The closer we got to the house, the more nervous I became. What would I say to them? What would they say to me? I didn't have to worry too much about that, though. After asking for their forgiveness, I was amazed at how readily and fully it was granted. I'd like to say that this was the perfect end to my story. It wasn't, however for the first time in my life, I realized what it meant to have unconditional love. These Godly, loving people were my family. Each one of them had every right to disowned me and cast me out of the fold, but they didn't. They were giving me a taste of what God's love must be like. My heart was finally just a little softer.

I stayed with my family while I slowly focused on preparing myself for life as an independent adult. When that time arrived, I was certainly better prepared thanks to my father, mother, and siblings. On my own, I found a job and a small apartment. It was time to set sail into adulthood.

# Chapter 12:
# Is That All There Is?

Just like the song that Peggy Lee escorted to the top of Billboard's Easy Listening chart in 1969, I began to wonder if this endless cycle of frustration, anger, and disappointment would follow me all of my days. Being an adult was no easier than being a toddler, child, or teenager. The specifics changed, but the overall theme remained the same. Is that all there is?

Life was hard. In some ways, it became even harder. I worked hard all day, every day. When the paychecks came, any level of satisfaction was smothered by what was left after I paid my rent, the bank note on my car, and all the other typical bills that everyone sees such as the money needed to buy groceries, electricity, and fuel for the car. At the end of a "good" month, I only had sixty dollars for discretionary spending. In hindsight, I could have, and should have started saving it for those rainy days that come in everyone's life, but that wasn't the case. My leftover money was wasted on cigarettes and clubbing, often returning to my apartment drunk. It's amazing I was never caught for DUI.

My sister and mother knew all of the places at which I spent my free time. To this day, I don't know how they were able to find that out. Knowing what they did, they checked up on me often to see if I was okay. Whenever the opportunity arose, they would invite me to family gatherings, many of them around the holidays. I would also periodically go to church with them as well. I was continually amazed with the unconditional love and patience they gave me. It was truly the only glimmer of fleeting joy I experienced as I wandered from odd job to odd job, making barely enough to survive.

My social life in the dance clubs was only a front. Anyone bold enough to dig a little deeper would have seen an intensely lonely man. I had no meaningful friends. No one I knew wanted to hang out with me. Why would they want to? I was always casting a negative aura wherever I went. I was journeying through my early adult life with "me, myself, and I."

The flicker of hope from my family forced me to think that, perhaps if I spent time reading my Bible and praying more often, things would change. During those times in prayer I would persistently ask God why I was the way I was. Why is it that I could not be happy about myself? If God was trying to break through to me, I couldn't hear His still, small whisper to my spirit. As I look back, I clearly understand that I may have been trying to reach out to God, but my heart was truly not behind the effort. Just like my nightclub scene, the whole thing was just a front. I wasn't fooling myself. Satan still had a hold on my life because I let him.

My odd jobs were never steady. There were periods when I lost my job. Suddenly, with no income at all, I could not pay my bills. At times, this meant that I would sleep in my car. During those cold and lonely nights, my thoughts would gravitate to the family that God gave me. I often entertained the idea of driving to their house where I know I would have received a warm welcome, but guilt would wash away those thoughts. I loved my sinful ways more than I hated the life it was giving me.

Somehow, I learned of a place in a nearby town that gave people in my situation some stability. It was a conservation job program in my area. The administrators provided the work, a place to call home, along with decent, balanced meals every day. I ran into so many other young adults just like me, people who had no place to go and in many cases didn't really know how to care for themselves.

It was a judgement-free zone where all of us could learn how to change our way of thinking in order to teach us how to be stable, contributing members of society. We were taught many helpful skills, like how to build a boardwalk or how to build a children's playground. All the while, we had a place to call home, personal guidance, and three square meals. After two years, I learned enough life skills to graduate. I had a kind of confidence I never experienced before. I was better prepared for the world at large. It was time to move back to the place I called my hometown.

Two steps forward, and three steps back. At times, any glimmer of hope from forward progress was only thwarted by new challenges. New challenges and temptations were always there, but new chapters in my life brought them up to the surface. The world at large was very effective at pushing them just when I thought that things were getting better. My eyes were tempted by things inside adult stores. My body craved alcohol and cigarettes. There were even times that I found myself taking hits from marijuana being passed around by people I didn't even know.

Smoking cigarettes was second nature to me. My brother got me hooked on them when I was only eight years old. Eventually, I started developing migraine headaches from smoking too much, but the nicotine addiction prevented me from quitting, something I tried over and over again without success. As the migraines worsened, I finally came to a point-of-no-return. Either quit now or suffer irreparable, permanent damage to my body. For a reason I can only attribute to God, I quit cold turkey without any quitting aides. It was one of the hardest things I have ever done, yet quitting cold-turkey is the only way I could have successfully navigated that goal.

I may have had success with giving up cigarettes for good, but I was doing my best to draw satisfaction for my flesh from anywhere, but it always ended up in disappointment, self-anger, and deep shame. Here I was, an adult, and nothing had really changed. Anytime thoughts of ending my miserable existence came, instead of fighting them off, I coddled them and gave them serious thought. All the while, my family and friends were fighting on their knees for me. Despite not knowing that, those prayers prevented me from doing myself any harm. God kept me alive.

Sinful living doesn't really mix well if you are a Christ-follower. God sees every secret thing and is privy to every secret thought. The Holy Spirit was always convicting me of my sinful habits, but I also knew that it was driven out of God's immeasurable love for me. It was one of the bright rays of light that seemed to occasionally break through the monotony of my daily existence. Those moments were fleeting, but enough to keep me marching ahead, holding my breath trying to figure out when the next low moment would be.

By the time I was in my mid-twenties, I had essentially hit rock bottom. That isn't saying much, though, since I spent so much time in life's valley to start with. How does someone "go lower?" By spending all of one's waking time thinking about the years of heartache, pain, sadness, abandonment, fear, and struggles. Spending time alone didn't help. I had no one to lift my point of view. I was a "bottom feeder" and I was sure that I would always stay there. The brief periods of joy and happiness I felt when I came to America and when the Wilsons adopted me seemed like an aberration. Did that really happen? I was now doubting it.

Yet, when I looked around me, I did see happy and joyful people, but they were all off in the distance. Getting back any semblance of anything good seemed like a fairy tale destined only for princes and princesses. I falsely believed that I was cursed to live a life in the deep dark valley. I had essentially given up. I missed the last train to anywhere decent. If it wasn't for the intercessory prayers being laid at God's feet from my family, I'm convinced that my plans to end my earthly existence would have succeeded. How could God ever have any kind of plan for me?

I couldn't see past the chains that I wore of my own free will. You see, all through my life, I never forgot the people in my journey who have hurt or offended me. Every moment of unforgiveness was simply another link on a very heavy chain that seemed to get longer and longer with every passing day. All of the grudges I held became a kind of security wall that was so high and thick, that I became a prisoner inside my own walled world. Strangely, I felt comfortable there and did little to reach out. All the while, my friends and family persisted in praying for me.

That lonely, isolated place that I called "my life" was about as dark as it could possibly get. Getting used to the darkness wasn't an option anymore, but how was I going to escape the thick walls I built around myself? How could I possibly take the heavy chains of unforgiveness off of my arms and legs? The task seemed impossible… and it WAS impossible, for me.

# Chapter 13:
# Love Breaks Through

Without so many people interceding on my behalf in prayer, I would be dead. In fact, I should have died long before leaving South Korea. God is not a God of time and saw the prayers of many before they were even offered. Even if I didn't see it at the time, God was seeing me through every horrific chapter so that someday, I could minister to others who might be going through a deep and treacherous valley.

In hindsight, working through all of these dark chapters would have had a different result without my family and friends who were all so concerned for my well-being. Hope is so much easier to sense when you are not doing life alone. I truly understand how hopeless someone would feel if they were navigating through tough times alone.

In many other ways, my adopted parents had experience with navigating through numerous trials. They were married when they were very young. When two high school graduates go from school books one week, to man and wife the next, they automatically run into challenges that rise to a completely different level. Despite that, both of them loved the thought of being surrounded by many children, and so God gave them the desires of their hearts five times over. (Besides the five, Mom carried a few other babies in the womb, but miscarried. We all know they are safely with the Lord in heaven, waiting patiently for a reunion someday.)

Their love for children went far and above a simple love to bring a lot of children into the world. God gave them a heart for special needs children. Over the years, they identified children who needed special attention and adopted several of them. Every single child's circumstances and needs were different. Without fail, they stepped up to the challenge and went to work helping each child grow into the person God created them to be. The obstacles were as wide and different as the east coast is different from the west coast. My adopted brothers and sisters had challenges that ranged from being paralyzed, to autism, to an infant whose inner organs developed on the outside of the body, to developmental issues from a birth mother who was a drug addict. Each child was completely different, but the way my parents addressed each circumstance always started with extravagant love. They had no favorites and loved each child the same.

We all had enough to eat every day and we all felt the love they had for us. As they move into their golden years, it's fun to see them operate the same way with the eighteen grandchildren (and one great-grandchild) that surround them often. I wish I could have appreciated all of the sacrifices they made in order to bring us all up. In hindsight, I am in awe of what they went through. None of it was easy, but one steadfast element of growing up Wilson was that they never, ever gave up on any of us. They recognized that God had a special purpose for each of their children and they weren't afraid to tell us that. I can honestly say that I returned to church life because of how they lived. I know full well that they prayed for me daily. Many of my friends did the same, too. Despite the number of times I turned my back on all of them, they forgave me each time. They modeled the grace of God offered to humanity through Jesus. Surely, I thank God for all of the good people He put in my life.

My father and mother, the Wilsons, were given a mission during their lives together. They accepted and loved me unconditionally for who we were. It was the same with every other child they both had and adopted. They could have given up on me a very long time ago, but they never entertained that idea. I always had a place to call home, a place where I had a father and mother who held out arms that were wide open. As I gain a lifetime of increasing perspective, I now understand why God chose this family for me.

Even now with every child either married or living on his or her own, the Wilsons still look for ways to serve others, in the community, at church, or anywhere. With such a strong bond of family love, is it any wonder that all of my brothers and sisters congregate at their house for holiday dinners together? I often pray and ask God to allow our time together on this side of eternity to be long, full, and complete.

# Chapter 14:
# Hope And Strength

Hindsight is an amazing thing. Navigating through each trial brought one thing into sharper and sharper focus: What I truly needed and what I didn't.

What I did not need: Counseling and medicine. Please don't misunderstand me here. There is a place for counseling, and there is even a place for medication in the role of lifting anyone out of a place of despair. However, what I really needed was a touch at the core of who I am. There is only One Healer who can reach that place: God. That makes total sense in hindsight because I know that He uniquely designed and made me who I am. Finding a good Bible-believing church also helped my victory, since I was surrounded by people who could keep me focused on the Creator who loved me dearly.

It's fair to ask me why turning to God would be the key to changing the direction of my life. Once more, the reason came into focus after I received the grace and forgiveness that He offered. Only then did I realize that, while He received me "as-is," He wanted to transform me like a caterpillar transforms into a butterfly. God's Word tells me to "therefore be imitators of God" (Ephesians 5:1 NASB). If I'm being called to imitate God, the first step is to think like God. After decades of thinking my own negative, defeatist thoughts, changing that wasn't something that would happen overnight like I would have wanted.

While that transformation is still taking place to this very day, I can tell you that reading my Bible every single day began to show me how to protect my thoughts from going off the rails and into a quagmire of where our arch-enemy wants us to be. Without that daily Divine guidance, Satan would have been successful at controlling who I was becoming, leading me farther and further away from the One who made me!

Imagine the outcome if nobody would have given me the Good News. I would have never known that the Creator of the universe was ready, willing, and able to give me the tools I needed to crawl out of the deep, dark hole in which I was living. I'm forever grateful that someone told me about Jesus and how He was reaching toward me with His powerful arms and hands to pull me out of a hole I had no hope of climbing out on my own. I also am forever grateful for the intercessory prayers offered by so many people of faith. All of this hope and strength to do what I was not able to do continues even to this day. My Lord carried me out of the abyss, and he guides my steps on life's journey. Once my focus shifted from my circumstances to keeping my focus on my Lord's guidance, and committing to following His lead, everything seemed to slowly start coming together.

Part of that process was enrolling in college in a trade in which I was not only interested, but good at! For two years, I studied drafting. Up to that point, it was the most challenging thing I had ever set my mind to accomplish. Working full time while enrolled in a degree program wasn't easy, but I earned my degree with God's help. I remember that period well. It was 2001. In September of that year, I remember getting the news that the United States was under attack by a group of radical hijackers. I felt personally attacked. The USA was my home! I joined many others around me in crying, especially for the thousands of people who lost loved ones. The strange mix of great sadness and great joy come together when I think of the period in which I finally reached a significant academic goal.

After graduating with my degree in drafting, I found a part time job in my new craft while I worked full time at another place. I knew this arrangement would be temporary, so I set my mind to do both jobs well until I could move to drafting full time. That made waiting for my next chapter easy. The wait was only a few months before I was able to move into a full time drafting job. I had to move closer to that job, but that was not even an inconvenience when you genuinely enjoy what you do for a living. It was yet another part of my life starting to come together.

While I enjoyed music, exploring that world was not even a distant thought. With my world perspective brightening, and with the luxury of a little free time, I picked up an instrument that I was drawn to - a violin. There are many that say that a violin is one of the most difficult instruments to learn and master. They are right, but because I love the sound, my mind was made up. As hard and as difficult as that violin was to play, I practiced as often as I could. Eventually, I was able to offer my violin playing to the Sunday worship group at First Friends Church, and eventually at Grace Community Church in Massillon. Some of the worship songs were difficult to learn and play, but my fellow music teammates always encouraged me in my desire to make it sound the best it could be.

By now, my circle of friends was broadening with the kinds of people that God prepared to come alongside me. When I think of how misguided many of my so-called friends were, and how quickly they were leading me down the path of destruction, I would have every right to be angry with them. But I adopted God's way of dealing with that. I learned to forgive them totally. I will leave judgement to the One who is the righteous judge.

The closer I got to God, the more peace I had in my spirit and the more strength I had in my heart to walk in a way that pleased Him. Had I never decided to receive the Good News of Jesus Christ, I fully know that I would be dead by now, entering eternity without God. Praise God for this new direction. Despite all the good things happening, and despite all of the good, Godly people around me, a part of me was still incomplete. I felt alone. I dreamed of being a husband and a father. I wanted my own family. I asked God for a wife and kids in prayer every single day, sometimes every hour. I had no idea that God was working silently on my behalf.

# Chapter 15:
# Could It Be?

Just when I believed that my fortune had turned and that my life journey was finally being kind to me, a chapter in my life that should have been filled with satisfaction and joy was eventually heading to a set of unseen class five rapids, something for which I was completely unprepared. Initially I was happy to find still waters.

My life was peaceful. I was active in church life, playing my violin in the orchestra. I was also creating artwork that I would display and sell at a local, annual arts and craft show. I moved out of my apartment and rented a guesthouse out in the country and continued to work as a drafter, drawing plans for private pools and projects for a water park company. Professionally, things were coming together, but personally, I was still envious of others my age that had the love of their own family surrounding them.

I found a little local bookstore that I spent my weekends perusing books and sipping on coffee. In the back of my mind, I was hoping that I would meet the woman of my dreams there. Despite my loneliness, I sensed God telling me to be patient as I prayed to Him and asked Him to direct me to the right mate. As often as I went there, nothing happened. I began to wonder if my Asian appearance was a hindrance to meeting that someone special. Little did I know that I would have better success in a place I hadn't really thought of.

Every Saturday, I took my dirty clothes to a laundromat in Louisville to wash my clothes for the week ahead. One particular week, after loading my clothes in a basket and heading to the laundromat, I thought about turning around and washing my clothes on Sunday. I didn't really feel like doing them that day. After a little hesitation, I decided to plow through something I didn't really want to do at that moment.

When I arrived, there was one other girl washing her clothes. At first, I didn't say anything. I focused on the task of cleaning my laundry for the week. I noticed that she was studying something, so after my clothes were securely in the washer, I sat beside her to sit and watch the television that was on. Normally, I would be so shy that I would not say anything to initiate a conversation, but this seemed different. Without much thought, I asked her what she was studying. She responded that they were books on teaching.

At first, the banter was very slow. Eventually, it became more interesting. We finally exchanged names. Let's call her "Dagny," (not her real name). Dagny then asked me if I went by any other name because I looked familiar to her. That caught me off guard. I mentioned that "Jon Wilson" was my adopted name from an adoption that occurred when I was 18 years old. I told

Dagny what my given name was before my adoption. I could tell that she was thinking hard. As our conversation progressed, we discovered that we had gone to middle school together and that we were in art class together! She told me that all of our mutual classmates called me the "art kid," because I was so good at it.

Soon, we started talking about all kinds of things, like jobs, family, and life. Our conversation was so engaging that each of us forgot totally about our laundry. After quite a bit of time there, and with all of our laundry dried and folded, I didn't even give second thought to giving her a hug. Dagny gave me her telephone number so we could stay in touch. I walked out of the laundromat smiling at how I met a nice girl, not at the bookstore, but at a laundromat!

One evening some time later, I called and asked her what she was doing. Her plan was to grab a bite to eat at a local Taco Bell, then watch a movie at home by herself since all of her children weren't going to be home. She then asked me what I had planned. Since it was nothing exciting, I asked Dagny if she wanted to grab something to eat and watch a movie together at my place, which is exactly what we did. Both of us enjoyed not being alone. Even though we were both nervous, this "date" was nothing more, something with which we were both okay.

I found out quite a bit more about Dagny. Her past was studded with many challenges including abusive relationships with one former husband and two ex-boyfriends. One of the brighter spots included her four children. Over the days and weeks, I became a present force in her life. When she needed a friend to walk her through a time that included medical attention, I was there. We were both enjoying getting to know each other, slowly and without pressure.

Our casual dates seemed to always be at my house. It took a long time before she invited me to her house. I soon understood why. Her family's living conditions were sadly nowhere near where they should have been. Her former husband and boyfriends took little interest in making sure they were taken care of. Without going into detail, let's just say that the list of what needed fixing was incomprehensible. As a single mother of four children who had to work to feed her family, regular house maintenance items that most of us see as compulsory were unchecked for so long that small issues became insurmountable. Despite the living conditions, her four children seemed polite, kind, and happy. I tried helping as I was able, but there was no way everything could be corrected without plenty of outside help. Despite all of these challenges, we all started to gel together. Could this mean a future for us long term?

The following Valentine's Day, in the presence of Dagny's four children, I proposed. I also asked her four children if they would be happy if I married their mother. Not only did Dagny say yes, but so did the kids! We were all floating on cloud nine. Finally, my own family to cherish and love, along with a family that loved me.

After we announced our engagement to our parents, everyone around us became joyful and helped us with all of the wedding preparations. We decided on having the wedding at my parent's church in Massillon. We felt like this was going to be a great place to grow in our faith together as a family. It all came together like a glorious dream. So many people from the church volunteered to weave together a storybook wedding day for us. We thanked God for everyone since we were both somewhat clueless about how to plan the kind of wedding day that was both beautiful and within our budget.

The time between our engagement and our wedding seemed like a blur. One day, I woke up and our wedding day had arrived. Everything was in perfect order, even the weather! Bright sunshine lit up the sky all day. It was as if the sun was focusing a beam of light on all of us. My bride was stunning and the kids were all dressed up and happy. The church began filling up with all of our family and friends. I chose my brother to be my best man and Dagny's best friend was her maid of honor. In all of the hustle and bustle, several thoughts hit me seemingly all at once. The first was that I was about to become a married man, something I believed would never happen. That thought would have ordinarily released thousands of butterflies in my stomach, but another thought took over. As I looked ahead, I smiled to think that I could put loneliness behind me. When the Pastor introduced us as Mr. and Mrs. Jon and Dagny Wilson, there was great joy in my heart.

# Chapter 16:
# Discovering The Sweet Spot

Up until that moment, the vast majority of my day-to-day life consisted of a never-ending waterfall of negative thoughts and emotions about myself and of the world around me. Fighting off this negativity was an exercise of futility. Instead of exhausting myself with the attempt, I simply wallowed in it. All of my problems and issues were "not my fault." I would always blame others for my deep depression. Until recently, it had never crossed my mind to ask for help. I had always had to rely on myself for my survival. Beginning with my journey as a street kid in Korea, it was the only mode of operation I knew.

I thought that I was "fine," even when others saw my need and tried to help. My emotional scarring was so deep that prescription medicines only covered up the depression and anger I harbored. Counseling would only scratch the surface, then attempt to spread frosting over my deepest inner turmoil. If the truth be known, I was comfortable with all of the hurt because it was all I really knew. I easily became angry with those around me, and because I was angry, I no longer cared how badly I hurt other people along the way. I had a scorched earth, "misery loves company" attitude.

I'd love to say that it all changed in an instant, but it did not, even after I responded to the Good News of Jesus Christ. My heart and soul were so hard and damaged that patient Godly people and God Himself gently worked on leading me to a much better way. I had to learn how to let offenses go. I had to learn how to truly forgive others. I had to learn how to allow myself to love other people. Only with a new heart of flesh to replace my heart of stone (Ezekiel 36:26) would this be possible, but with God, ALL things are possible (Matthew 19:26)!

Hindsight is always much clearer. Knowing how much more quickly my life would have improved with God, my only regret is not running to God sooner. Trading in my past for His brighter future for me softened my heart. The deep-seated anger I loved to harbor was no longer ruling my heart. It was dethroned by the King of Kings, Jesus, who showed me how to replace that anger with great love. He did that when I started dining on God's Word. The more I read, the greater my appetite became for His Word. Every answer I ever needed was found in its pages. Every single one.

Allow me to pause here for a moment to affirm God's Word by my testimony. The Bible is the world's best-selling book with over five billion copies printed over the centuries. While anyone can certainly purchase a copy at any local book retailer, there are also plenty of places at which you can secure a personal copy for free. Reading it is only the start. Believing what is in its pages will then lift anyone out of bondage of any kind. God's Word will free us from deep pain and suffering from the past, present, and future. Life on Earth is too short. Time wasted on living life without God will only frustrate you in the end. Living life _with_ Jesus as Lord and Savior will prepare you for an eternity with God in heaven when your body dies. It's never, ever, too late to ask Jesus into your heart and to, once and for all, send our mortal enemy, the devil, packing. When I did that, it was as if I said: "Hit the road, Jack. Don't you ever come back no more, no more, no more, no more!"

The church doors were still open and waiting for me to enter. It was there that I was surrounded by people who genuinely loved me and gave me the guidance I needed to grow in my faith. Don't misunderstand me here. I'm nowhere near perfect. I often neglect praying like I should. I don't read my Bible as often as I should. The devil and his band of cohorts are real and they trip me up when I am most vulnerable. While it's true that they cannot ever pluck me out of God's Hand (John 10:28) or take away the salvation Jesus gave me, when I sin against God, it clouds my testimony for Jesus. That's why it's important to me to have a church family. After confessing my sin to God and repenting (which means to turn direction), the Scriptures tell me that God is faithful and just to forgive me of ALL unrighteousness

(1 John 1:9). My church family then surrounds and encourages me to live a more Godly life.

Unless you surround yourself with God's Word and with Godly people in a Bible-teaching, Bible-centered church, relying on therapists, counselors, or prescription medications will only serve to bandage a much deeper problem called sin. Only the One who created us can really free us from the deep hurt and emotional pain that often drive us to do things that drive us further from God, our Healer!

I'm more confident about the future than ever before, not because life is smooth and sweet. It often isn't! Because I am in the palm of God's Hand, I can not only walk across the glorious mountain peaks, but pass through the valley of the shadow of death (Psalm 23) knowing that I will never be alone. Jesus Christ IS _my_ Lord and Savior. He now lives inside and through me, my ever-present help (Psalm 46:1).

My wife and I started attending my parent's church, a place filled with loving people who loved the Lord with all of their hearts. The Lord could not have led us to a better place to grow in our faith. It wasn't a big place (I think we would have fallen through the cracks if it was). Every single member made us feel important and needed. We immediately started plugging in and helping where we were able. I joined the praise team and played my violin. I was even encouraged to play a few solos during some of the Sunday worship services. The pastor saw that I had a gift for relating to young people, so he eventually asked me to become their youth leader. My wife and I were able to engage the youth and teach them how to live a full, Christian life. We planned many fun outings, all with the focus of instilling Godly principles and values to the youth under our care.

As we grew in our faith and prioritized our commitment to our church family, our sense of joy and life purpose grew in ways I could not have ever imagined. Many of my obstacles still showed up in my life journey, but now I had the heavenly tools to either navigate past them or to put them under my feet. Those obstacles no longer defined me. Living my life for God defined the purpose for my life, the purpose I had often doubted without His Divine perspective. I quickly learned that all the things that too many people set their hearts on, self, money, fame, or "things," are all temporary and only satisfy the flesh which will never truly be satisfied.

As I look back, I see and experience God's unfathomable patience in waiting for me to turn to Him. My bottom line advice to everyone is that it's never too late to invite Jesus into your heart. He stands at the door [of your heart] and knocks (Revelation 3:20). He will never force His way in, but what He will do is be persistent in waiting for you to open up the door to Him. It's also never too late to go back to church. For me, it was where I learned more and more about the grace I received from God and can't recommend finding a Bible-based, Jesus-loving church enough.

While my new spiritual tools still help me to navigate in a fallen world, the fact remains that obstacles of all shapes and sizes may surprise any follower of Christ while we are journeying on this side of eternity. After a season of great personal and spiritual growth, some of life's obstacles were too difficult for a married couple to successfully navigate unless both attacked those obstacles with joint, resolute commitment. Sadly, my journey as a married man and father, something to which I looked forward and envisioned for a lifetime, came to an unanticipated conclusion. Despite my objection, I'll readily admit that there's enough blame that we both shoulder. Nothing could ever prepare someone's heart and spirit for an unwanted marriage dissolution. I won't sugar-coat it. It hurt deeply.

While there were days that felt as if God abandoned me, I leaned on the Bible passages that told me that God would never leave me or forsake me (Hebrews 13:5). I gave higher priority to God's Word than my own feelings, something the devil will try to use to drive a wedge between God and His adopted children.

# Chapter 17:
# The Road Ahead

If you made it this far, you know how crazy and unpredictable my life's journey has been. That's where God's patience and grace takes over. The longer I live, the more understanding I have of why God intervened to keep me alive so many times. It certainly isn't anything I did, rather it's all about what His plan was and is. Every now and then, God pulls back the curtain of His reason and His purpose for my life. Instead of dreading the next day or week or month, I truly see a glorious future.

What changed? A lot, but it all came down to only a couple of key things. First, I stopped listening to Satan, my arch enemy. Once I did, I could then hear the voice of God. My heart, once a place of continual stormy tempest of the worst kind, became a place of smoother sailing and more gentle winds once Jesus arrived into my heart to reside. When Jesus is in your heart, fear and worry disappear. As long as I maintain my focus on Him, I have complete peace and satisfaction. This is where I want to stay for the rest of my earthly journey.

One of my favorite Bible verses is one that is quoted often and for good reason. It's John 3:16. It says: "For God so loved the world that he gave his one and only Son, that whoever believes in him shall not perish but have eternal life," (NIV) to which I respond with a grateful, "Amen!" It's one of the verses I cling to when life's struggles and heartaches try to steal the joy of my Godly identity. The reason I am still alive today is because God shielded and protected me from everything that should have killed me long ago. He saved me from many dangers, not the least of which was myself and I can't praise Him enough!

Years ago, God planted a dream in my heart to write a book so I could encourage others that are facing similar struggles. God placed the right people in my path to help me make that happen, but it did not happen overnight. There were days, weeks, even months when it appeared as though the process had screeched to a stop. God was still moving to make things happen even though I could not see it. Now, here we are!

It's my prayer that you are reading my story at God's appointed time for you in a way in which all of this makes sense. May your faith be bolstered as you lean on God and have greater faith and patience than I did. Learn from my mistakes. Better yet, imitate my joy found only in the saving grace of Jesus Christ, my Lord and my Savior. Don't let the devil and the world rob you of the joy of being an adopted child of the living God.

Just a few more things. Love God with every part of you. Praise Him every day. Praise Him every time you think of God's goodness anytime it crosses your mind. Next, love those people around you, your family, your spouse, your children, and then your friends, workmates, and acquaintances. Also, love your enemy as Jesus commanded. Jesus also asked us to take care of those who are less fortunate. When you see someone who needs a hand, jump in and help. Be truthful. Do all these things without being distracted by the world. The devil uses such things to lure our gaze off of Jesus. By staying focused on and imitating our Heavenly Father, you are building up great treasure in heaven, a place where there is no decay (Matthew 6:20).

We may be redeemed and adopted by the One True Living God, but while we are journeying through life, we still operate inside a fallen body, capable of sin. Be quick to turn away from sin (that's what the word "repent" means) and ask God for forgiveness. He is faithful and just to forgive us from all unrighteousness (1 John 1:9)

Remember to enjoy everything that God created. Look up at the sky and marvel at how God paints on His canvas. Look at trees, birds, butterflies, and the ocean with awe and wonder. Draw strength from seeing God's creative power and take great comfort in knowing that heavenly help is on the way. God is never late. Ever!

I may not know you personally, but I am earnestly praying for you! May our eternal destinations be the same thanks to Jesus.

May the Lord bless you and keep you. May God watch over and protect you and your family. Go with peace in God, allowing Him to direct your steps so that you will prosper in everything you do. Praise Him! Sing to Him! Let it loose and let it flow! Release heaven on earth until the day Jesus returns to gather His Church. Amen.

"Greater is he that is in you,
than he that is in the world."
1 John 4:4 (KJV)

Made in the USA
Middletown, DE
25 September 2022

10925079R00066